A View from the Top

MARGARET JENSEN

HARVEST HOUSE PUBLISHERS
Eugene, Oregon 97402

Scripture quotations are taken from the King James Version of the Bible.

Cover by Left Coast Design, Portland, Oregon

A VIEW FROM THE TOP

Copyright ©1997 by Harvest House Publishers
Eugene, Oregon 97402

Library of Congress Cataloging-in-Publication Data
Jensen, Margaret T. (Margaret Tweten), 1916–
    A view from the top / Margaret Jensen.
        p. c.m.
    ISBN 1-56507-570-6
    1. Christian life—Anecdotes. 2. Christian life—Meditations. 3. Jensen,
    Margaret T. (Margaret Tweten), 1916–   . I. Title.
    BV4501.2.J436 1997
    277.3'082'092—dc21
    [B]   97-2663
                                                                        CIP

Printed in the United States of America.

97 98 99 00 01 02 / BC / 10 9 8 7 6 5 4 3 2 1

Dedicated to my grandchildren . . .

that in the years to come, when I have a box seat with a view from the top, they will remember the truths they have heard me speak and watched me live to the best of my frail ability.

I want them to know that I will be Home—waiting for each one to be at the table for God's Sunday dinner.

- ❧ Heather Dawne Carlberg Willis, married to Matthew David Willis (my new grandson); they are in medical school in Philadelphia at Temple University.
- ❧ Chad Judson Carlberg, a graduate of Gordon College and a true communicator of life and humor in his own creative way.
- ❧ Christopher Shawn Jensen, who works with his father Ralph in "The Master's Touch," creating eighteenth-century masterpieces.
- ❧ Eric Lund Jensen, soon to graduate from King College in Bristol, Tennessee, then marry his college sweetheart, Clover Musick. (I will add another granddaughter to my family.)
- ❧ Sarah Elizabeth Nightingale Jensen, a student at the University of North Carolina, at Wilmington, North Carolina.
- ❧ Kathryn Elise Jensen, who attends high school in Wilmington, North Carolina.

Special Thanks

This gives me the opportunity to thank my family and friends around the world for the love and prayers that follow me across the miles.

🌹 There is always the agony and ecstasy of life, but the ecstasy for me is to travel with my daughter Jan Carlberg to share the truths of God's Word through "faith lift" stories that bring generations together. (Jan's husband, Dr. Judson Carlberg, president of Gordon College, forgets I'm 81 and sends us off with his blessing, and, "Mom, you can do it!" So— I believe him!)

🌹 When I come home from a long trek over the miles and see the faces of those dear to me—Ralph, my son, and his wife, Christine—waiting to bring Mama and her suitcase back home to a cup of tea and a prayer of thanksgiving for a safe journey, I know the ecstasy outweighs the agony of life.

🌹 Looking over the dear faces around the Sunday dinner, I give thanks for each one in his or her place. Sarah always sat beside Papa. Now she sits beside Ralph. Thanks be to God.

🌹 There are many who make the yoke easy and lighten the burden of everyday living, and I thank Harvest House Publishers for including me in their family.

🌹 Thanks to faithful Linda Britton, who can look at a computer and actually smile.

🌹 Thanks to Billie Holt for "driving Miss Daisy" in rain or shine; she can remember where I'm speaking and "gets me to the church on time."

🌹 A special thank you to Esther Fieldberg from Canada, who gave me the title "View from the Top" in her Christmas letter. There she tells of her statesman husband, a respected patriarch with a full white beard, sitting at the Thanksgiving table after a serious stroke. With tears he sang the Doxology and said that the past year had been a long, hard climb, but the "view from the top is great." What a witness to faith!

My prayer is that those who come behind us will find us faithful. Thanks be to God for His unspeakable gift!

Contents

1

The Safe House

Within the hollow of a cave, the mountain of stone cradled a simple frame house and red barn. From the rocky ledge the cottage looked down from the mountain to the clear-flowing fjord. There was only one view—the forward look, with towering mountains overlooking the narrow arm of the sea that ran between the walls of stone.

Protected from the storms, the sturdy cottage looked snug and safe. For a moment I imagined that I was part of that safe house, just a speck surrounded by the majestic beauty of Norway, the Land of the Midnight Sun. Patches of green revealed garden spots for food, while down the mountain the fish swam in the cold, blue water. Hidden in the cleft of the rock of my imagination I dared to dream of a long-ago time when my people came from the Land of the Midnight Sun.

In the cave of my imagination I wondered if there had been a little girl who looked like my youngest grand-daughter, Kathryn Elise, with long corn-silk hair and deep blue eyes. Perhaps there had been a "Katie" with a vivid imagination, who curled up on a rocky ledge and dreamed of faraway places beyond the mountains. Did she dream of writing books or of putting the mountains, sky, and sea on canvas with her brush and oil? How often did she descend the stone steps to fish with her father or climb back to tend gardens, goats, and chickens? Could she have dreamed that down the corridors of time someone would sail in ships to the then-unknown world called America?

Today our Katie knows that her great-great-grandparents came to this land and that I, her "Grammy," was the first in the Tweten family to be born in Woodville, Wisconsin, USA, in 1916.

Today I look into the next century, the year 2000, and back again over the years. Somehow deep within me I desire to face Home—not the little house nestled in the arms of stone, or my lovely home surrounded by flowers, but the Home where the Father has a prepared place cradled in the arms of His love. I may not see the next century, but I will see my eternal Home.

We speak of the valley of the shadow of death, but I see the mountain of hope, with the lights of Home reflected over the rocky climb. Generations have preceded me; friends and loved ones waved goodbye with a sigh and a smile—a sigh to leave the familiar but a smile of hope for the eternal. It's been a long climb, these 80-plus years; faith sees my eternal Home more real than my lovely home of brick and wood.

With the morning dew still on my roses I open the screen door to walk into the morning sun. From the patio swing, with my coffee cup in hand, I watch the squirrels and dog chase each other across the green grass. In the brisk ocean breeze I watch the pampas grass waltz in the wind, while the palm trees bow gracefully in a French minuet. The sassy daisies with bold dark eyes jitterbug to the music of the early morning. Birds in the treetops sing their song and keep the orchestra off-key.

Periwinkles, my favorites, look up at me with gentle faces that say, "We'll be here, the last to leave when winter winds blow—but come spring, we'll arrive early." Faithful—always faithful! Sun, wind, cold, rain, or heat, their faces look up with a smile. "We are here for you."

The roses wilt, the gladioli bend in the storm; even the sturdy marigold turns brown; the geranium needs attention; the happy red salvia get discouraged, and their petals fall. Not my periwinkles! They greet me with *faithfulness*. Up and down the mountain of life, into the valley of broken hearts, up the rocky climb, over stumps and briars, the periwinkle people keep coming—climbing, falling, stumbling, sliding, they keep coming.

How God must love the periwinkle people—the *faithful ones!*

I put my coffee cup down and walk along, pulling a weed here and there, toward the 45 yucca bushes I planted along the road. The prickly yucca serves a purpose, to keep out stray animals—a fortress of pricks, but not for a centerpiece.

Talking to my Doberman, Scout, is a front for talking with Harold, my husband of 53 years, who died several years ago. I don't usually tell that, but it is true. Walking through the garden I ask, "Do you remember when we planted 30 holly bushes—look how they have grown!" (He remembers.)

"Remember how we planted the azaleas in pouring rain, then dug holes for the pampas grass we got on sale for $1?" (I'm sure he remembers.)

"Look at the palm trees and how they withstood the hurricane." (I'm sure he peeked between the clouds.)

"No one is around, so I can talk to you, Harold. Sometimes in the evening I cry—especially when I sit at the piano and sing the old love songs: "Oh how I miss you tonight, miss you when the lights are low. . . ." That seems to be the hardest time, when I turn on the lights and close the blinds. I seem to see you in your leather chair.

"But they aren't tears of grief, guilt, or regret, just those 'missing you' kind of tears, because hope lets me see the lights of Home. I have two homes, Harold—the one you prepared on earth (and thank you for all your hard work, painting, and planting) and another Home where the heart lives."

With a thankful heart I walk away from the palm tree that bent and swayed under hurricane winds but stood up to welcome a new day when the sun came out.

I put my coffee cup away and open the door to my office. I have a book to write, miles to travel, words to pen—words of hope and courage for my grandchildren. My words may inspire faith, but only God's Word will be a lamp and light up the rocky mountain road into the next corridor of time—the year 2000.

2

The Wedding

A golden glow filtered through the stained glass windows of the historic Christ Church in South Hamilton, Massachusetts. Snow-covered overcoats and boots were discarded in the foyer while handsome ushers waited to escort the elegantly dressed guests to the pews of the stone church. Across the glistening fairyland, organ, trumpet, and voices traveled on the winter wind. It was December 29, 1995.

With a mischievous wink, my number-one grandson, Chad Carlberg, lovingly tucked my arm in his and seated me in the second row. I waited alone. I knew my husband Harold had a box seat from the grandstand of Heaven, while angels echoed the back-up music.

On the arm of her son Chad, our daughter Janice Dawn Carlberg was seated beside me. We clasped hands. This was no time for tears, but memories raced for priority ratings on the backroads of my mind. Sitting beside me was Jan, the mother of the bride, elegant in velvet. But to me, for a moment, she was "my little girl." Where did the years go?

It seemed only yesterday that she filled our arms and hearts with joy. School days ran together: Madam Alexander dolls, a blue uniform to wear in the marching band (she played trumpet), piano lessons, and frilly recital dresses. The years ran into each other. Then it was Wheaton College, where she met Judson Carlberg. Tonight she sat beside me to bless the marriage of their only daughter, Heather Dawne Carlberg, to Matthew David Willis.

Somehow I think Matt's mother, Irene Siebens Willis, was sitting beside my Harold, Heather's beloved "Papa," watching from the portals of Heaven—their view from the top. I could almost see Papa take Irene's hand and whisper, "Isn't God good to bring Matt and Heather together? If you tell me about Matt, I'll fill you in on Heather."

Heaven! Home! Land where no tears are flowing—only beauty and peace. Heaven, where preceding generations are waiting at the end of the road, at the top of the mountain. Home!

Coming through the mist of time I remembered how my father, E. N. Tweten, blessed his first grandchild, Janice, and called her his "Princess." Later, when he met Jud, he said, "Oh ja, I see the Princess has her Prince." (He was right!)

Where did the sunsets and sunrises go? In my heart and album I hold a picture of my father blessing the tiny Heather, cradled in his arms—his first great-grandchild. Now he watches with Mama from their Home.

Then there was the day when Dr. Robert Carlberg dedicated his beautiful granddaughter, Heather, to God.

Great-grandparents, grandparents, aunts, uncles—all surrounded this child with love and prayers. I'm sure that Matt, too, was encircled with love and prayer.

Perfection didn't come through the genes of past generations, for there were tears and sorrows, and challenges that didn't always get the best choices. But they were not errors of the heart, for the heart didn't leave home—the heart of God and His grace and mercy. Goodness and mercy followed them all the days of their lives and now they dwell in the house of the Lord forever.

The godly seed of generations past would find fertile soil in the hearts of the young; for love, tears, and prayer would continue to break up the fallow ground and prepare the soil to allow seeds of righteousness to grow. Down through the generations comes seed from godly French Huguenots who stood firm in biblical convictions; the seed from stubborn "faith of our fathers" Scandinavians; the seed from "how firm a foundation" English—all met through the corridors of time to find fertile soil in Matt and Heather.

Preceding generations prayed for their children and children's children to come, that all would serve the true and living God through faith in His Son, Jesus Christ. God's answer to those prayers ascending to His throne is the promise that He will bless them that fear the Lord; they and their children will be blessed of the Lord (Psalm 115:13-15).

At the trumpet sound I was brought back to the present. We stood to watch Heather, on the arm of her father, Dr. Judson Carlberg, president of Gordon College, come slowly down the aisle. Matthew, with a stray lock over his forehead, waited with boundless joy etched in his face.

I thought of the triumphant marches I had witnessed when Jud heard the band play at the dedication of the Gordon College chapel; the awesome inaugural ceremony when men of God knelt to bless the new president. Now Jud walked sedately, with his beautiful daughter on his arm; the trumpet didn't sound for him, but in celebration of the wedding.

I wondered what he was thinking. Did memories race on the backroads of his mind? Was there a tinge of sadness for the passing of childhood, too soon gone? There was also joy in believing that God brought two special people together—as one.

"Who gives this woman?"

My thoughts were brought back to the moment. Somehow in my heart I heard God whisper, "I do."

My heart answered, "Matt, she is a treasure from God; cherish her well."

He will!

As man and wife they knelt at the altar. "This is My body broken for you. This is My blood shed for the remission of sin. This do in remembrance of Me." One by one we followed them to the altar and knelt together—a time of communion with God and man.

The trumpet and the organ rang out from the historic stone church across the glistening December fairyland. Husband and wife joined family and friends for a celebration of joy. Past snow-covered fields the cars moved slowly to the Mansion at Turner Hill where the beautiful reception was held.

Heather and Matt graciously mingled with the guests; at the close of the festivities, Matt suggested a songfest around the piano where Christmas carols blended joyous voices with trumpet and piano.

Over the winter wonderland of New England, I'm sure the angels heard us singing their song: "Joy to the world, the Lord is come!"

3

The Wedding Dress

While we were packing our bags to return home after Heather and Matt's wedding, we heard weather reports that a New England blizzard was on the way. It took two vans to get us all to the Boston Logan Airport, where my sister Joyce and her husband Howard were returning to Arkansas. The rest of us—Ralph, our son, his wife Chris, their children, Shawn, Sarah, Katie, and I—were heading for North Carolina. Surrounded by baggage and long lines we said our goodbyes and departed to our gates.

Fourteen-year-old Katie settled in beside me. "I'm sorry that my brother, Eric, couldn't get out of school, but I'll tell him all about the wedding. I wonder who will be next?"

"It's difficult for me to think that my first grandchild is married. I'll always think of you all as our little girls."

"To think she was married in your wedding dress! I can't believe they are going to Turkey, then South Africa to work in a hospital. I think I'll go to Norway on my honeymoon."

"Knowing you, Katie, you'll probably do just that—go to Norway—and you'll be a beautiful bride, just like your mother. She had a Christmas wedding, and the bridesmaids wore green velvet. Maybe you'll wear her dress—or you could wear my dress. Oh well, we have some years to plan that one. I just hope I live long enough to see it, but I may be watching with your Papa from his box seat in Heaven. Either way—I'll be there! You can count on it!"

"You'll be there, Grammy; you'll live to be 100. Aunt Jan says she's putting your name down for Willard Scott on "The Today Show.""

"Leave it to my little girl Jan; see, she always will be my little girl, even when she's 50 years old. The older I get, the younger they all seem.

Well, I have news for all of you," I said. "I plan on living *forever*. That's the great news! Sometimes I think there is a fine veil that separates the visible world from the invisible. My Harold always seems to be near. Someday we will know!"

"What's the story about your wedding dress, Grammy? Is it true that it cost $13?"

"That is true, but it cost a small fortune to have the heirloom dress cleaned and the tiny rust spots from the covered buttons removed, plus the lace in the train replaced or repaired. A creative seamstress near Boston does that intricate work of restoring treasured wedding gowns. On her walls are pictures of 'her brides' in historic gowns. Now that gown is protected in a plastic bag for the next wedding."

"To think we used to get your wedding dress out of the cedar chest and play wedding. We clumped around in your satin shoes; so much fun, especially on a rainy day. Even Heather used to play 'dress-up wedding'—then she wore the dress for her real wedding. No more 'dress-up!'"

"Before I tell you about the dress, Katie, I have to go back to a long-ago time when my father was the pastor of the Logan Square First Norwegian Baptist Church in Chicago. In my father's church there was little age distinction, and we called the older people 'Tanta' (Aunt) or Uncle; we were all part of a family where the social life centered around the church.

"As high school students we often studied together in the library, played tennis, had winter skating parties, and celebrated each other's birthdays. About ten or 12 of us worked very hard—chores at home and part-time jobs—but when we played, we played!

"Most of the members of my father's church were immigrants from the Scandinavian countries. Everything was new—the culture, the language—but the church was the center of their lives, where faith was eternal and God's love never changed. There they were secure—their safe place. You know, Katie, everyone needs a safe place—home and the church. That was my safe place as a teenager, where the older people prayed for us and took an interest in everything we did.

"There were the 'Tantas,' who managed to scrape up a nickel for an ice cream cone during Depression years. One beautiful white-haired 'Tanta' bought a new coat for my high school graduation gift. Another friend, Leona, took me to Marshall Field's and bought my first store-bought dress, high-heeled shoes, and silk stockings. I thought I was Miss America. And one elderly tailor completely renovated an old coat to look like new. That was the language of love that we understood in spite of the broken English. That red brick church seemed like God's loving arms reaching around His family in the new world. His love was old and familiar—no language barrier.

"When your Papa and I decided to get married, my father had accepted the pastorate of the First Norwegian Baptist Church in Brooklyn, New York, after serving many years in Chicago."

Katie's head fell on my shoulder, and I wrapped my arm around her—a long day! When I looked around they were all asleep. Oh well, this was a good time to remember. Besides, I'll tell it all again. Somehow it gets to be easier to remember the past than to keep up with the hurried present.

I put my head back while Katie slept on my shoulder. How I wished I could cradle them all on my shoulder and wrap my arms around them—to give them a secure nest. Deep in my heart I knew that only God's arms of love wrapped around my children could be their "safe place."

Then I went back to a time in my father's red brick church on the Square. I was working at Lutheran Deaconess Hospital in Chicago while Harold was a student at Northern Baptist Seminary. My salary was $80 a month, and I managed to pay back $300 to my mother. She had cashed in an insurance policy to get money for my books and uniforms when I entered Norwegian American Hospital nurses' training. Now I had to save for my wedding.

In the meantime Harold worked at Bunte Candy Company, besides attending school. He managed to save money for a car, wedding, and furniture for our three-room bungalow apartment on Central Park Avenue. We were rich! (I must remember to tell Katie all this when she's awake.)

I had to chuckle to myself when I remembered how Harold walked to work and brought his lunch; the big extravagance for us was a five-cent icecream cone. But we made it!

We decided to be married in my father's church in Brooklyn so all my family could be a part of the plans. I knew I would miss my homechurch family in Chicago.

Ruth, a friend of Mama's, said she would help me to get a dress. Now my church family got excited. They all knew Tanta Ruth's ability as a seamstress and a bargain hunter. That's how we ended up on Maxwell Sreet, Chicago, where shopping, yelling, and bargaining were an experience.

Merchandise was out in the street where merchants and shoppers were yelling and bargaining, laughing, and telling jokes. One favorite joke was told about a customer who kept yelling, "Cut the price! Cut the price!" The merchant agreed. When the man got home with his bargain trousers, he found that the pants had been shortened. Furiously he returned to the merchant. "Look, look at these pants—like short pants!"

The merchant scratched his head. "So you cut the price—I cut the pants."

I had heard about Maxwell Street, but this was my first adventure. Then we found it! Tanta Ruth was triumphant and held up her intended purchase—an elegant ivory satin dress with lace inserts in the train and tiny covered buttons down the back and on the sleeves.

"Thirteen dollars!" Tanta Ruth was in her element. "Now ve go for the veil." We did! Two dollars! Then the satin slippers for $1.98.

There were no secrets in my father's church, so everyone knew about Tanta Ruth's triumph. A group called the Ruth Society consisted of the Norwegian women of all ages, but they were affectionately called the "Rut Girls." They thought I belonged to them—after all, we were a family.

I couldn't help but think how sad for young people to belong to their peers or gangs when it is security to be part of all ages where wisdom and experiences are shared. I was the youngest, but I learned from the older "Rut Girls."

Now the Ruth Society decided to have a party and a mock wedding. I was to model this famous wedding gown from Maxwell Street. (I must remember to tell Katie all this.)

It was so many years ago, but I can see their loving faces and their work-worn hands as they stroked the soft satin gown. Most of the "girls" worked as domestics, and many never married. There was no bitterness or jealousy, only a love for their family—me. They presented me with a lovely gift from the "Rut Girls"—a beautiful hand-knit blue Afghan, one I still use.

"Come, now ve have reception!"

The coffee was poured, and delicious cakes and sandwiches had been prepared. Somehow I always remember the Swedish limpa with goat cheese, those special openface sandwiches with hard-boiled eggs and anchovies. Such a long ago time—but no one could set a table like those Scandinavian immigrants. Somehow they brought a touch of the homeland with them, with their herring and cheese—and especially the strawberry cakes with real whipped cream.

I wonder how many unshed tears hid the dreams that never came true. Could it be that they saw the wedding dress, worn this time by Heather, come down the aisle from their view from the top? Could it be possible that they would remember the "Rut Girls' party" and the wedding dress more than 50 years later?

I must remember to tell my children to tuck away the molten moments deep into their hearts. There comes a time when memories bless the quiet years.

When we went to Brooklyn, we discovered that my father's church was a "family," and there was excitement because the pastor's daughter was coming to their church to be married.

Uncle Joe, my mother's brother, built an arch and decorated it with blue hydrangea flowers. My sister Grace was the maid of honor; Doris, my sister, and Fern, Harold's sister, were bridesmaids; Joyce was my junior bridesmaid; and Jeanelle, the youngest, was the flower girl.

The colors were peach and blue, with bouquets of Talisman roses and blue larkspur. (I must remember to tell

Katie, when she wakes up, that all my sisters were at our golden wedding, where Chris and Jan planned the same colors of peach and blue. They even had my $13 dress displayed on a mannequin.)

Oh, dear, that reminds me of my parents' golden anniversary when Mama had her picture made in her lace wedding dress. My father's passion in life was books. He took the money put aside for wedding pictures and bought books.

My angel mother understood! "Oh ja, so he must have books—so I wait."

Fifty years later she had her picture. I couldn't help but think how love covers a multitude of faults.

Katie stirred in her sleep and murmured, "I think I heard you talking to yourself, Grammy—but I fell asleep."

"Don't worry, honey, I'll be telling it all over again."

Looking out the plane's window I watched the billowing clouds in the deep blue sky and wondered where Home really is—just a step from earth?

Someday there will be a wedding dress for each one—a robe of righteousness—that robe a gift from God. "For God so loved the world, that he gave his only begotten Son, that whosoever believeth in him should not perish, but have everlasting life" (John 3:16).

God paid the price, but to us who believe it is a gift.

"Fasten your seat belts. Welcome to the New Hanover International Airport." We were home; the storm was left behind in New England.

There would be other storms.

4

The List

Returning from New England to a desk of mail and the to-do list was like leaving a beautiful mountaintop to slide down a bumpy road into the valley of the ordinary. On my desk was the calendar marked with retreats and conferences in faraway places: Canada, Florida, the Carolinas, Texas, Boston, Seattle; interviews, appointments; and then that never-ending list—travel agent, taxes (ugh), dentist, vet for Scout, leaking faucet, broken porch light, more bushes, shampoo carpet, cleaners—mail, mail, mail!

I remember hearing that "the glory of tomorrow is rooted in the drudgery of today." I wasn't too sure about the glory of tomorrow, but I had a good taste of today.

How I missed Harold, who good-naturedly zeroed in on details and kept the routine of the day from becoming drudgery. He kept the lists checked off. Instead I seemed to only add more tasks to them.

In the quiet of the morning hour I stopped to ask for directions for the day from my Heavenly Father, who could help me to keep my priorities in order.

He did! As I sit at my desk I chuckle to myself when I recall how that prayer was answered.

"How lucky can you get, Grammy? You'll never be alone again. I just moved into the garage!" said Chad.

There hung my bed sheets to partition the sleeping area from the computer and exercise equipment. Clothes hung neatly from rafters; on the metal garage slides was a surfboard. (I must *not* open the garage door.)

"Grammy—never fear! Your grandson Chad is here!"

Believe me, humility is not one of my number-one grandson's spiritual gifts, but his effervescent good humor and wit can turn a rainy day into sunshine.

"Don't forget, Grammy, I had a landscaping business during college years—so out go those ugly bushes to the back fence." With boundless energy he tore into the landscaping business of my yard, washed windows, shampooed the carpets, fixed the light, and took the dogs to the vet—I had to go to the dentist myself.

Oh, yes—dogs! Gus the German shepherd joined the family, and Scout and Gus became allies in digging up flower beds and standing tall at the gate to warn intruders.

"Grammy, you have it made—and you do love me, don't you?"

I reached for my list and added:

1. Attend Chad's plays.

2. Never run out of peanut butter and jelly.

"Yes, Chad, I love you!"

This number-one grandson graduated with honors from Gordon College, where his father, Dr. Judson Carlberg, is president. His zest for living out the creativity that God put in him brought him into a world of drama, art, writing, and surfing—that was part of Wilmington, North Carolina. I knew that was step number one, and I wondered where God would plant step number two.

Chad's famous comment is, "If Grammy dies, I get Scout. If Scout dies, I get Grammy." That is how it stands!

When the night comes to cover us with a blanket, a shield from the cares of the day, I usually pick up a book and read a few pages before turning out the light.

I picked up a book by Michael Phillips and read:

> In all his purposes for the world, the Creator allows time to help accomplish them. Whether it be an individual heart, in the relationships of a family or nation, time teaches, heals, strengthens, deepens roots and gives perspective. God is not in a hurry. His plans are never rushed.

I closed the book, turned out the light, and pondered how God's ways are not our ways.

When a new day dawned I put on the coffeepot—another routine day, with the desk of mail and list waiting. During my Bible study I opened *What the Bible Is All About* by Henrietta Mears, and continued my study of the prophets. For some reason Ezekiel caught my attention, for he was Chad's age when he was brought to Babylon as a captive.

Daniel had been brought there a few years earlier, and one of our favorite Bible stories is about Daniel in the lions' den. God honored his faithfulness, and he ended up in the palace—a true "rags to riches" story.

Ezekiel lived by the Chebar River, a ship canal, that branched off from the Euphrates above Babylon, the most beautiful city in the world—with palaces, gardens, temples, and bridges—the showplace of the East. While Daniel lived in the palace, Ezekiel probably dug canals with the Jewish captives. The Jews had no temple; national life was gone; they had little opportunity for business.

"A nation's troubles are the result of national apostasy from God." This was the message given to Ezekiel, who was able to dramatize to the captives the visions God revealed to him. Not only was he an actor but also an artist as he painted the revelations with words of judgment, warning, hope, and God's glory. For 22 years he dealt with the discouraged captives and told how the Messiah would come, then return again with power and great glory.

God used Daniel in the palace—but he also used Ezekiel with the captives digging ditches.

For a moment I wondered how easy it would have been for Ezekiel, with all his creative talent, to be lured into the lifestyle of the beautiful Babylon with all its glitter and gold. He remained true to God.

In my heart I could see from my view of 80 years how my creative grandson could be the teacher of art, drama, creative writing to a culture holding our youth in captivity. Then again, that was only my plan, and in deep humility I must stand back and watch how God will plan the next step.

I wondered how we transmit truth to our children. How do we bring the life of Christ into a culture hostile to biblical teaching?

Out of the mist of time I saw the face of a man whose white hair framed deep blue eyes—a man who walked with God. Mr. Mason lived a life of learning, teaching, loving, and serving. The broken people came to him, and he sat with them until they could stand, then stood with them until they could run life's race.

Mr. Mason was a gentle man of God who started a prayer meeting in order to pray for all the pastors of Greensboro, North Carolina. It grew from three people to over 100 people.

When all my efforts to bring changes in others seemed to fail, I cried out in frustration to him, "What do you do when even love fails?"

He looked at me tenderly, without rebuke, and answered quietly, "We can make decisions only for ourselves, Margaret. Only God can change hearts. Love never fails."

Now Mr. Mason is Home, his view from the top; he knows what he saw by faith.

I must remember that it is the life of Christ in us, poured out into the marketplace by the power of the Holy Spirit in everyday obedience to God's Word, that reaches out to those around us. Not our words—our lives!

Faith and works go together; now I had to tackle that desk with the list—and mail.

The telephone rang! "Peter and I are going to the Bahamas for a missionary conference."

"How wonderful, Jeanelle. I usually go to Florida in August or Toronto in December." We laughed together; the joy of having my sister live near me was an unexpected gift from the Lord. For years the miles had kept us apart, but our hearts never moved and now we could be in the same town—and reach for the telephone.

Jeanelle had been the pianist at the First Baptist Church, Ft. Lauderdale, Florida, for 25 years. God brought Peter Stam and Jeanelle together—a beautiful love story—then they moved to the Washington area. Peter, a renowned missionary statesman of the Africa Inland Mission, became the missions director at the Fourth Presbyterian Church, Bethesda, Maryland. With quiet dignity they moved among the political figures, the lonely, the elderly, and extended their welcome to the strangers from a far country.

Jeanelle's gracious social skills, gourmet cooking, and beauty of godliness combined with Peter's missionary heart to give their guests an enjoyable experience in warm hospitality. The love from this great church followed them to Wilmington when they retired.

Now they were going to the Bahamas and I would miss them—but there was the desk with the endless list to tend to, a reminder that faith and works really do go together.

The days had a way of turning into weeks when a phone call crashed into my world. Jeanelle and Peter were home from the Bahamas and on their way to the hospital. That was the day when time, calendars, and the list stood still.

A storm swept in—*cancer!*

Nothing would ever be the same. The five seemingly invincible sisters felt a break on the heart. Across the miles the hearts and hands came to build up sandbags of faith against the incoming tide.

I closed my office. The list would wait.

5

The Triumph of Faith

We need a miracle!" The sisters wept together. If only we could change places!

"She's my mom!" The grief-stricken children, Robert and Charlene, clung to each other.

"Not my Aunt Jeanelle—so much to give!" The cousins huddled together.

"Not my sweetheart, the precious gift from God who brings such beauty and love into my life."

The intensive care unit did not look like a miracle to me—tubes, bottles, the hum of machines.

The young cried out in fear, anger, frustration, and pain. The cry heard throughout the ages rang out in the night of sorrow. "Why?"

Across the room Peter's white head was bowed in grief; he who had known trial, sorrow, and loss reached to the throne, beyond the hills, from whence his help came. For him the cry was not "Why?" but "How?"

Through the years of dusty roads, rocky climbs, hills of challenges, and valleys of sorrow, we who have traveled long have learned that God's people live on the promises of God—not explanations. Someday we will understand; so will the young as they keep traveling life's road.

"Oh, God," our hearts cry out, "have we taught them well?"

The answer comes back gently, into our spirits. "I will instruct them and teach them in the way they shall go. I will guide them with My eye."

Across the miles came a card from an unknown friend. "When I found this verse, you came to mind." On a beautiful card were these words: "Watch yourselves so that you do not forget the things your eyes have seen or let them slip from your heart as long as you live. Teach them to your children and to your children after them."

I keep the card on my desk.

The nights and days blended into a gray blur, but eventually Jeanelle came home to face new words like "chemo," "CAT scan," "blood tests"—and "hair loss" (not that beautiful blonde hair!).

Surrounded by loving nursing care and the support of family and friends, Jeanelle saw a glimmer of hope come like the early morning dawn as it slips from behind the night. Calls came from around the world where intercessory prayer groups brought God's special child to the throne of grace.

There were days when faith would mount up on wings; then a clammy claw of fear would pull the mind into a valley of doubt. On one of the "valley days" Jeanelle cried out, "I need to hear from the Lord—some word to hold to." We wept together and I promised to go to the throne for a word.

"I'm asking for a miracle."

While my hands were plunged into the routine of the day—making beds, hauling down garbage cans, washing dishes, loading the washing machine—my heart cried out while tears mingled with prayers. There were meals to prepare, so I put a roast in the oven—all the practical duties that must be done to keep order with family and friends coming and going.

Suddenly I stood still in my kitchen, dried my hands, and lifted my heart in one cry. "Oh God, we need a miracle!"

I stood still. A deep peace covered me like a blanket and then I heard—not a voice—but I heard: "Faith is a miracle!"

Out of the long-ago past came the words of an old hymn that we sang in my father's church in Chicago:

Encamped along the hills of light
Ye Christian soldiers, rise. . . .
Faith is the victory . . .
That overcomes the world.

I ran to the living room and found an old hymnbook and *shouted*, not really sang, all the verses. When I picked up the phone I could hardly speak. "I heard, I really heard that 'faith is the miracle.' To believe against all we see is a miracle, for that kind of faith comes from God. Now we have a theme song—'Faith Is the Victory.' Let's sing it to the world!"

I reached for the phone and called Janice, my daughter and prayer partner. She had been weeping before the

Lord. "Not my Aunt Jeanelle—don't let the music die. *The enemy won't win!* Jesus, You are able to do abundantly above all we can ask or think." She answered the phone.

"Jan, I heard! Faith is the miracle."

We sang over the telephone, "Faith Is the Victory."

Down the list I went—my sisters Joyce, Grace, and Doris; our beloved pastor Horace and his wife Tennie; the Nelsons in Seattle; friends and family. The next thing I heard was that churches were singing our song; the word went out: "Faith is the victory!"

Two weeks after surgery, March 30, was Jeanelle's birthday; it was also Tennie Hilton's birthday. Once again I reached for the phone and called Marie, the special friend from Florida who was caring for Jeanelle. "Put on the coffeepot, Marie! We are going to have a party! Jeanelle can rest on the sofa, and Horace and Tennie are coming. I'll bring the lunch."

With car keys in hand I drove to Harris Teeter Grocery and ordered from the deli what was needed. "How fast can you decorate a cake?"

"Right now! What name?"

"Faith is the victory!"

The young lady stopped. With tears in her eyes she called another clerk. "Look—just what I needed to hear."

"Me, too—everything has gone wrong today."

When I went to check out, the older man bagging groceries said, "Oh, look at that cake. My mother is very ill—I need to hear that."

People in line leaned over and with tear-filled eyes echoed, "I needed to hear that."

When I reached the Stams' house the table was set. Horace and Tennie pulled up. Jeanelle was propped by pillows and sat at the table.

We sang "Happy Birthday." The candles were blown out. Together we sang our song, "Faith Is the Victory."

Across the miles the messages of faith came: "This is for the glory of God; if you can believe, you'll see the glory of the Lord."

The young were watching! They saw the sandbags of faith hold back the incoming tide of fear and doubt. The young heard the triumph of faith—before the battle was finished. They, too, are singing our song.

"Faith is the victory that overcomes the world."

6

The Tie That Binds

Through a mist of rain, my plane slipped into its parking place, and with my bag in hand I headed for the U.S. Air Club. I had a three-hour wait for the plane to my favorite destination—home!

A gray weariness, like the rain, seeped into my bones, and I found myself slowly moving toward a good cup of coffee and a cinnamon bun. Every place was filled. While I balanced my tray I heard someone say, "We are leaving."

With a "thank you" I slid into a seat and slowly sipped my hot coffee and munched on a bun.

"Excuse me, may I sit with you?"

"Please do." I moved my tray and made a place for a young man.

"Where are you going?"

"Brown University—Providence, Rhode Island."

"Oh, how interesting! My granddaughter Heather and her husband, Matt, graduated from Brown and now are in medical school at Temple in Philadelphia."

"You must be very proud."

"Oh yes, I am, and I'm sure your family is proud of you."

He looked at me and added, "There is a special bond between a grandmother and her grandchildren. I just came from my home in Birmingham, Alabama, where I visited my grandmother—she fell out of a wheelchair. I have a deep emptiness inside of me, a gnawing fear of losing her before she sees me graduate. She only had a third-grade education, and it's because of her and my mother that I am a student at Brown.

"Our family is very close and when one hurts, we all hurt. My mother finished high school, and my grandmother and mother are wise women. My dream is for them to see me receive my diploma."

I forgot my coffee, and my young friend forgot his hamburger as he poured out his love for his family and his loneliness in a culture without a biblical worldview.

"Without the teaching from my mother and grandmother I would have a difficult time standing true to godly principles."

Suddenly the weariness ebbed away, and a glow of love for this young man warmed my soul. While we sat at that table in the center of airport traffic we had our own "church"—a time of sharing eternal truths and a promise to pray for his grandmother.

In my hand I held his address, then reached up to hug another adopted grandson. When he wrapped his strong, black arms around me he whispered, "I love you"; then he was off to Terminal C and I turned to Terminal B.

Once again I marveled how God brings people together and prayed that somewhere, sometime, someplace there would be a grandmother who could reach out to one of my grandchildren when they felt an "emptiness in my heart."

After speaking several times over the past weekend I felt drained, tired, and ready for my own pillow—home. Out of the mist of rain and weariness the sun came out in that young man's handsome face—a face that could have belonged to my precious Lena, a symphony in black. The deadline for my new book, the schedules that seemed to run the airports didn't seem important. Two hearts touched! A grandmother and a grandson.

What was it he said? I must remember—oh yes. "I thought knowledge was power, but when I told that to my mother she said, 'Oh no, knowledge is a tool. If you believe that knowledge is power, then you will be led to arrogance; but if you believe knowledge is a tool, then you will serve. There will always be someone with more knowledge, so use what you have in service.'

He also said, "One day some classmates mocked Easter, Jesus, and the resurrection. I just said to them, 'You believe all the books you study, and take exams, so you believe in something. I have chosen to believe the Bible.'"

I pondered his words and turned my heart to God. "Oh, God, let me live to show your glory to the next generation. Teach me your way—then let me give it to others. Bless my friend." I knew we would keep in touch, and I'll send the *Lena* book to him.

Where did the three hours go? Time to board for home.

7

The Bean Patch

There are some things you have to give up, Grammy. Shawn and I will be in college, so there is no one to help with the garden. Keep the flower beds, but let's plow up the garden and plant grass seed. After all, you can go to the farmers' market."

Deep in my heart, I knew that Eric, my grandson, was right, but I wanted everything to be the same. It wasn't the same! Harold was "Home"!

That was five years ago.

It was the bean patch I kept seeing in my mind. Harold used to remind me to put a string from stake to stake, but I would get in a hurry and drag the hoe in my imaginary line—not too straight, I discovered later.

It was Shawn I was remembering, who at three years of age was my shadow in the garden. I told him, "I'll make the holes and you can drop in the beans."

He held the Kentucky Wonder beans in his pail and carefully dropped the seed in the hole, his blonde head shining in the sun as he bobbed between the rows. We watched for the ground to crack open and then, finally, a green sprout dared to pop out.

Harold planted hills of squash and cucumbers and dug holes for tomato plants, but Shawn and I tended the bean patch, where my crooked rows showed up. Potato plants were in bloom, onions stood in a straight row (Harold's work). Even watermelon seeds found a home.

Later, Eric would sit beside me while I cut the potatoes for planting. How he enjoyed putting the potatoes in the hole—until we discovered Yenta, the yellow Lab, dug them up. We did the potato patch all over again.

Day after day we watched the garden grow. We dug potatoes for supper, fried the zucchini squash (called our "ministeaks"), and sliced cucumbers and red tomatoes.

Shawn and I liked to pick the green beans before they were too big—just the right size. Later, Chris, his mother, and I filled the freezer with string beans.

Ralph, my son, liked the old Southern beans, cooked all day with fatback—the kind you have at homecoming, with dinner on the grounds and all-day singing. Chris and I cooked the beans lightly and added a touch of butter with salt and pepper.

There was a time when Eric, sitting in his high chair, didn't like string beans, so I put the beans on a plate with ketchup and whispered the magic words, "Green French fries!"

He ate the beans.

Shawn was not impressed. "Why do I have to use a fork and Eric uses his fingers?"

"Shh—green French fries!"

The day came when Eric caught on and used a fork.

One day Shawn and I sat on the swing and I told him a story about a boy who wanted to go fishing with his friends.

"You have to plant the beans first, then you can go fishing."

The father left him with the can of beans. The sun was hot, and the boy wanted to run to the pond. Suddenly he had an idea and dumped the beans in a hole; then he showed the father the empty can.

"Good, son! Now you may go fishing."

The sun and rain fell on the garden, and the seeds began to sprout. Up came the squash, peas, vines—but where were the beans?

Over in the corner of the garden was a clump of beans sprouting through the ground.

The father looked at the bean patch; then he knew why his son had finished so quickly.

About that time a group of neighbor boys came over with their fishing poles.

"I'm sorry," the father said, "Johnny will be busy planting beans."

That was a long-ago time.

Today I'm watching the grass over the bean patch and the pampas grass blowing gracefully in the wind. Shawn appeared—all six feet, four inches of him—and sat down beside me on the swing.

"You weren't talking to yourself, Grammy?"

"Oh no, I just talk to Scout." We chuckled together. "I was remembering how we planted the string beans and how Katie, three years old, planted grass seed. Everyone had a coffee can with grass seed, and we were having a planting party. Katie kept returning for 'more seed'; we caught on after the third round.

"Katie found a hole and dumped the seeds in it. In the corner of the garden we had a clump of green grass—Katie's garden.

"You know, Shawn, it is a reminder that what we plant doesn't always show up at once; it's called the 'law of the harvest'—what we plant is what returns.

"Disobedience to God's rules doesn't always show up at once. I read that the great sorrow is to pay for forgiven sin. God forgives when we confess our sin, but the law of the harvest still reaps the wild oats."

We rocked on the porch swing together.

"Sometimes it is hard to obey—but it is harder to not obey.

"I guess I have spent more time with you than the others; I was there when you were born. We used to walk around Lake Hamilton and talk grown-up talk—no baby talk to you—then we'd throw stones into the lake and watch the ripples.

"You were only two or three years old when you would stand with your feet apart, throw your head back, and sing like a performer, 'Bless the Lord, oh my soul, and all that is within me, bless His holy name.'"

"Oh, come on, Grammy, did I really sing that loud?"

"Oh yes, you sang to the ducks and geese as they swam gracefully across the lake. You used to belt out the part, 'Kings and kingdoms will all pass away, but there's something about that name.' You liked the 'kings and kingdoms' part."

We rocked quietly while I remembered a time of "childhood and toyland" that never returns again.

"One time when we walked along the lake you jumped up on a stump and wistfully asked me to carry you piggyback. I said, 'Of course, but why?' You were quiet for a moment while I carried you 'piggyback.'

'Uncle Dan used to carry me piggyback all the time so I could see all around up high. I miss him.'"

Shawn looked thoughtful. "That was 22 years ago, Grammy, and I remember and still miss him . . ."

"I miss him too, Shawn. We used to take long walks along the lake and talk about everything and anything. He was easy to talk to and was wise and understanding.

"He used to ride his bicycle from the beach where he lived to attend college at UNCW—right here across our road. We lived in Greensboro when he went to college. Harold and I would pack up food—roast, pound cake, cookies, and bring your daddy along for a weekend visit to see Dan. It was such fun!

"Although he lives far away from us, we always remember him with love—and we all miss him.

"When you were very young and building a farm with your Legos I heard you singing to yourself. You were only two or three years old—so I reached for a pen and wrote the words. I even remember the tune."

I love You, Jesus
I love You, Lord
I love You, Jesus
I love You, Lord.
I love Your flowers
The smell of Your flowers

I love Your bees
The hum of Your bees
I love You, Lord.

We rocked on the patio swing while I reminded him that he was a child of promise—a gift from God. "I looked up the meaning of your name."

Christopher: Vigilant in Christ; watchful one.
"Behold, the former things are come to pass, and new things I do declare: before they spring forth I tell you of them." (Isaiah 42:9)

Shawn: God is gracious; appointed of God.
"The Lord is my strength and song, and is become my salvation." (Psalm 118:14)

(*The Name Book*, Dorothea Austin)

"Your parents picked a good name for you, Shawn, and God has given you a free will to choose His way.

"Well, Shawn, Eric was right when he said I had to give up something, but I can keep the memories."

The grass now grows over the bean patch, and now I wish I had used the string between the stakes like Harold said so I don't have to remember the crooked rows.

I put my head on Shawn's shoulder. His strong arm held me close.

"I love you, Grammy."

It was a molten moment down memory lane—a view from the top.

8

Overshadowed

The pelting rain brought in by a true "Nor'easter" had the conference women running for cover to reach the dining room where hot coffee greeted the "storm refugees." I was drenched!

"Really, Mother, don't tell me you left your raincoat in the car—at home, that is!"

"I really did! Umbrella, too!"

After all, when packing in North Carolina sunshine it is difficult to think of raincoats. But I knew better! It had happened before.

Jan managed to get my wet clothes in a dryer, then wrapped me in a plastic tablecloth. "Oh, you look great, Mom! I'll use you as Mary in the Christmas pageant."

The tables were filled with happy women attending the New Jersey Keswick Conference where Jan and I were to share "The Generation Grasp." Discarding coats and umbrellas in the hall, the women came to a beautiful buffet where chefs in tall white hats served with a flair.

Tumbling through a dryer, my clothes were ready to swap the white plastic tablecloth for another rainy day.

Jan and I were there to share stories of God's faithfulness to all generations, but it seemed that amazing stories came back to us from the guests around the table.

Across from me sat an "angel" in human form—my friend Ellen. Looking back from my view from the top of years, I could almost see the young Wheaton student with curly blonde hair. For a moment I went back to the time Bud played the trumpet and "Overshadowed by His Mighty Love" seemed to come alive.

Then they were married—"overshadowed by His love"—and united in their love.

Ellen's claim to fame was that she beat Porter in Ping-Pong. Porter and his wife Irene kept open hearts and an open home to Wheaton students and strangers. They never made the headlines in the *Chicago Tribune*, but I have an idea there must be a "hospitality hall of fame" in Heaven. Porter tended gardens, and Irene stored food to be shared around a table filled with happy, hungry people.

After Sunday dinner with Irene's famous roast beef, apple pie, and cinnamon buns, Porter dared Ellen to beat him at Ping-Pong.

She did!

Now he is Home—and I wonder what he sees from his view from the top. I'm sure he sees what we see—two people, overshadowed by God's love, faithfully serving the Lord at home and overseas, then sending their beautiful children to the ends of the earth, sharing God's love.

Suddenly, Bud had a stroke! He is unable to read or communicate through speech, and Ellen has cared for him for 12 years. Slowly, though, he could sound out, "I love you!"

The blond curls have turned a soft gray, but when I looked into her beautiful face I saw beyond the weariness of aching shoulders to eyes filled with love and thankfulness to God for His faithfulness.

"I have wonderful children." Beside Ellen sat Martha, her missionary daughter, home on furlough.

The truly great love stories don't make *The New York Times'* best-seller list. They are the unsung heroes who keep love alive through commitment to God and each other.

"I love you" comes through the pain of lonely nights and weary days, and the love of God that overshadows us brings healing to a broken world.

God sees the process as the plan. Someday we'll sing together, "It will be worth it all when we see Jesus."

Across the table sat a dignified gentleman, the grandson of the man who had a dream—100 years ago. God took a broken man with a broken heart and made him a new creation through God's love—the gift of salvation through Jesus Christ, God's Son.

From the gray ashes of the past he built a monument to the glory of God. Not a monument of gold or stone, but a monument of men—thousands of men who found new life in Christ; with renewed hope they stretched their hands out into the marketplace in godly service.

How often God uses one person to become the length and breadth of a dream.

One hundred years ago—a dream! Today—a monument of changed lives. Across the years I seem to hear Bud's trumpet: "Overshadowed by His Mighty Love."

It was time to say goodbye to the beautiful conference people at America's Keswick; time to board another plane.

This time I was up at 4:30 A.M. to catch an early flight to Boston, where I was to speak at a former Swedish Baptist Church in Worchester, Massachusetts. It was the 100th anniversary of Grace Baptist—another dream in the early days of Scandinavian immigrants.

When the choir sang a medley of old hymns I felt a tug pulling me back to my father's church of immigrants in Chicago.

The strangers in a foreign land soon established a church—a safe place for the heart. Within 22 years the population of Swedish immigrants grew to 7,000, and eight churches were established.

The torrential rain continued, but nothing could dampen the festive spirit of the fellowship hall and a beautiful Scandinavian table. Then it was time to go home.

In the quiet morning in my own kitchen with my coffee cup I opened Oswald Chambers' *My Utmost for His Highest* and read:

> If I obey Jesus Christ in the haphazard circumstances they become pinholes through which I see the face of God—then I discover others who are blessed through my obedience.
> When God's redemption comes to the point of obedience in a human soul—it always creates.

If I obey Jesus Christ, the redemption of God will rush through me to other lives, because behind the deed of obedience is the reality of almighty God.

I need time to think about that—and another cup of coffee.

From a long ago time I think I can hear Papa's Norwegian string band:

Trust and obey
For "der" is no other "vay"
To be happy in "Yesus"
But to trust and obey.

When we all get to Heaven, our view from the top, we will probably hear Bud's trumpet in Gabriel's band playing "Overshadowed by His Mighty Love."

9

Hurricane Fran

Looking out the screen door of my office I watched the threatening gray clouds race across the Carolina blue skies, then turn into menacing black storm clouds.

The hammock under the lofty branches of my favorite maple tree swung precariously under the stately boughs. (I must remember to ask Katie, my youngest granddaughter, to pack up the hammock.)

Pines moaned while leaves and old branches fell to the ground. The wind blew a threatening, discordant sound—a preview of things to come. I knew I should tape the windows and make my emergency list, but my desk was piled with mail—so I let the wind blow.

When the evacuation order was given to the Wrightsville Beach residents I sighed for them, but I was inland. I kept writing.

Rain came in sheets! Time to close the office door and get a no-nonsense attitude.

The 11 P.M. news warned that Hurricane Fran was riding full force with the eye of the storm aimed at the Wrightsville Beach area. Tomorrow—Thursday, September 5, 1996—was Fran's schedule, between 4 and 10 P.M.

I went to bed. It had been a long day of writing in my office.

When morning came I shifted into damage-control alert and headed for my car to make the rounds: bank—" "no nonsense cash"; post office—the mail must go on! The car got special attention—full of gas, good tires—just in case of a hurried exit.

Harris Teeter Grocery was next, and it seemed to me that the entire town met there for old home week, filling grocery carts with bottled water, flashlights, and staples. Everyone seemed to have a hurricane story from past years. The lines were endless.

Finally I joined the bumper-to-bumper traffic and faced a stream of headlights coming from the beach areas.

In pouring rain I dragged my wet bags into the house. (I knew I should have done this yesterday.)

We could be without power so I put a roast in the oven and prayed for the "power, wonder-working power" to stay on.

Then the cars came: the red Jeep with Sarah, my granddaughter, at the helm; Ralph, Chris, and Katie, the youngest. A truck roared in—Shawn, number-two grandson; another truck—Chad, number-one grandson.

Before long another Jeep arrived, an "adopted" grandson—then a stranded girl with her dog and cat in a van.

That's when I almost lost it—three dogs and a cat in one house—later another dog and a stray kitten. When Chad answered the phone he said, "Jensen Hotel and Animal Shelter."

All the outdoor furniture, gas grill, garbage cans were made secure in the garage.

Scout, my gentle Doberman, forgot all her Southern manners and growled at the big lazy old dog who didn't know anything but to stretch out, wag her tail, and look at me with sad eyes.

Gus, the German Shepherd, enjoyed the attention of two females, so we had to separate "Old Faithful" from Scout; the cat stayed in the shadow of the old dog and knew enough to hide from Scout.

Later a puppy appeared on the scene and rode on the backs of the dogs—our own three-ring circus.

Marie, a new face in the crowd, blended in with an extra student, Christopher, then Nick and Melissa—then we stopped counting. Over the flooding and through the traffic to Grandmother's house they came!

My Chris and I flew into action, and the power stayed on so the roast was well done. New potatoes, cabbage, salad—all added to the table. Katie filled the glasses with ice and poured lemonade.

The men were glued to the news, but we finally made a "last call for dinner—before we eat in the dark."

Candles and flashlights were ready; Chris filled the bathtub with water to flush commodes—just in case! "Don't flush!"—the battle cry in hurricanes. We filled kettles with clean water and kept gallons of drinking water.

For a quiet moment we stopped to ask the blessing and pray for God's protection as people fled to safer places. (Jeanelle and Peter evacuated to Greensboro, 200 miles north.)

Just as we came to the dessert—ice cream and brownies—the power went off. Katie kept busy lighting candles and checking flashlights.

When the dishes were washed we gathered around the table again, while the wind screamed and the trees bowed to the power of the storm. It was an eerie feeling—warm, humid, and crying winds in the dark night.

Ralph read Psalm 91 and prayed for God's mercy and protection. Telephone calls came from all over the country, assuring us of their prayers.

Sitting by candlelight we played table games and listened to the wind. Before the ice cream melted we made milk shakes and kept nibbling on fruit and snacks while competing in Chicken Scratch, a game with dominoes.

The torrential rain and wind beat against the house. We knew the eye of the storm was close—a strange silence; then a roar, like a freight train plowing through the woods in the back of the house.

Then we heard it! A bang, like gunfire, and the cedars along our driveway fell like dominoes—all in a row.

The game was forgotten as we turned our flashlights into the murky darkness, then carefully edged our way to crowd up on the heavy patio bench to watch the drama unfold. I waited inside!

With a roar our towering maple tree was uprooted and lay sideways with the roots in the air. Too much water in the sandy soil, and the majestic tree crashed.

This was the tree that had withstood other hurricanes—the invincible maple tree, the tree that held the hammock—Katie's tree where friends and dogs took turns in the swing.

Papa had dug a hole for a sturdy post to hold one end of the hammock and drove a heavy hook into the tree. Now the branches filled half of the back yard and soon the beloved tree would be carried away. The lonely post stood in the rain—a reminder of what used to be.

Birds and squirrels had filled those branches, and under the shade the dogs stretched lazily to guard the house. Every morning a frisky squirrel called Henry came out of the tree to torment Scout. Just as our dog reached the hunted animal, the clever Henry jumped up on a branch and watched the frantic hunter.

I'm in the middle of a hurricane and wondering where "Henry" would find a new home. It's strange how we remember the small pleasures of life when suddenly they are gone.

How like the towering giants of the faith, seemingly invincible—like the powerful Samson or the conquering King David—then comes a molten moment when the roots give way.

We weep when trees with leafy branches that brought shade and protection in summer or winter are gone; like the passing of an old friend, a reminder of the frailty of life.

Another crash! We drew our flashlights and aimed at the sound behind the storehouse for garden tools.

With a roar the towering oak crashed and with it came the tree house that Shawn and Eric had built. I watched Shawn, 23 years old, six feet, four inches tall. "Grammy, my tree house is gone! Remember how I tied on Papa's carpenter apron that held nails and a hammer? Papa held the ladder and let me hammer away. We ate snacks and watched the world go by."

On life's road to the top I'm reminded that each one feels the passing of childhood in his own way. Sometimes we cry on the inside, but the tears don't show.

The eye of the storm had passed, and now the wind was left to cry through fallen trees. From a long ago time I could almost hear my Norwegian Mama say, "So—now we do what we have to do. Tomorrow is another day."

In the garage we pulled out cots and mattresses and opened sofa beds. The gentle old dog was whisked past Scout to be near her master in the den. The cat stayed in the station wagon.

Gus and Scout took care of the boys. Pillows and sheets came out of hiding and before long everyone had a place to sleep.

The night was dark and muggy with the eerie sound of crying winds. Exhausted, I found my own pillow and fell asleep. There was nothing more to do tonight, and tomorrow was another day when we would take inventory in daylight.

Candles flickered in the sink—a safe place.

I fell asleep with an old hymn in my heart. "He hideth my soul in the cleft of the rock . . . and covers me there with His hand."

My safe place!

10

Then Comes Tomorrow

Someone said that tomorrow comes before I'm finished with today. Tomorrow came! After a night of restless sleep we couldn't wait to see what daylight revealed.

It looked like winter had come before we were finished with summer. Trees stood naked in the morning sun, stripped of branches and leaves; even the swaying palm trees that bent with the wind stood with shredded fronds.

The sky was blue, the wind quiet, and a bird dared to sing; the dogs ran in circles in an unfamiliar setting.

"Come, jump in the car and let's see what happened to the shop and our house." Ralph gathered his crew, but I stayed home to fold up sheets and pillows and bring some semblance of order into the chaos. Someone had to watch the animals.

The morning was hot and humid, but I knew the crew would be hungry so I started the bacon and mixed up pancakes. Since the power was off I was thankful for the gas stove so I could feed this crowd. We ended up with 12 people, four dogs, and two cats.

From my shelf I took down my decorative Norwegian coffeepot and decided it was time for this fancy pot to do something useful, so I boiled the coffee in the old-time way of long ago. When my crew came home I bragged about my ingenuity to make real Norwegian coffee and brought a mug to Chris.

"Eek! There's a bug!"

My pride tumbled! Not only leaves blew in—but bugs came along.

"I'll take orange juice, please."

So much for my Norskie coffee.

"We took movies of our street." Ralph shook his head. "No one could believe the disaster, Mom. The huge door to my shop blew in, but we can repair that, in spite of all the rain. There is no power so no one can work. We lost four days of work during Bertha, so this is tough—but we'll make it."

"But Grammy, you should see our street where the ocean rolled in up to our steps and left seaweed all over. Ugh! What an odor! That's not all—here's a huge basket of clothes soaked in sea water.

"Grammy, don't you wash Shawn's clothes. He left them in the garage when he was supposed to wash them and bring them upstairs."

"I know, Sarah, but we'll manage." Shawn looked sheepish.

"You know that big house on the sound? Well, it's gone, and three houses on our block—gone! We are blessed, just some roof damage and water in the garage, but we have no power or water until an electrician checks out the damage; also the pump is damaged." Ralph continued to list the damage and made a call to the insurance company. It took two days to get through.

"You should see our yard," Katie continued. "A huge boulder in our front yard, plus parts of a pier and buildings."

Chad joined us from the downtown section where the Cape Fear River overflowed and water ran in the streets. "Last night there was a terrible crash. It was so frightening, and we found out it was the steeple of the big First Baptist Church. The pastor said, 'The steeple is gone, but we, the church, are here.'"

Ralph continued. "Remember my Simmons boat that sank miles away, but we recovered it? Well, the part that was missing washed up on my front yard. Can you believe that? I'm going to do something special with that part of my boat.

"No one can get to the beach; curfew and patrols are in effect. People are desperate to see if their houses stand, but many power lines are down, so no one can venture past the bridge patrols."

After pancakes and bacon, the Jensen crew and company was ready for the clean-up brigade.

Sarah told how they emptied refrigerators and freezers and gathered all the spoiled food into double garbage bags and placed them in containers at the end of the street for pickup crews. "What a mess!"

Sarah and Katie, armed with rubber gloves, Lysol cleaner, buckets, and rags marched to do battle against the results of Hurricane Fran.

Now was my chance! Everyone was gone!

I sat down to enjoy a cup of tea—no bugs—and read the paper. The headlines: "Fran called the worst in Carolina Power & Light history."

Resources seemed to come from all over America. "The Red Cross and grocery stores are giving water and ice." Schools were set up as shelters, and the homeless found refuge with relatives and friends.

"An elderly woman found floating on a mattress in the marsh." (She later died.) Phone lines were down, water was not safe to drink, and there was the danger of power lines tangled in trees.

While I gathered up the news, I wondered when we would get power; then the phone rang.

It was Eric from King College in Bristol, Tennessee; he was concerned about the family. I told him that we were safe but still had no power.

At that moment the lights came on and I screamed, "Power, we have power. Oh, praise the Lord!"

Eric laughed on the other end.

"I want to come home—sounds like a comedy."

"Well—it's no joke! But we'll make it. Now we can wash clothes—and flush!"

Eight loads of Shawn's ocean-drenched laundry were finally completed and folded in bags to go home—upstairs this time.

I knew Chris would scold, but that sea water was too much; besides, they were cleaning on Shannon Drive and I had to keep order on Oakleaf Drive. There would be more wet, soggy clothes from the rain, and it didn't want to stop.

I called my friend Billie and discovered that I was supposed to be at a committee meeting. "Well, we can forget that one! I'm having a convention of my own. But we just got our power on, and the house will be cool again. Believe me, my theme song is 'Power, power, wonder-working power!' What about Horace and Tennie?"

"They are here, but it is so hot and humid, and eating places are closed because of no water or power."

"Come over here! Tell Tennie and Horace my office will be ready for them—and you come, too."

My office! The place Horace Hilton, our beloved pastor, dedicated to God seven years ago. "Dedicate the bathroom." I laughed with them but said, "After all these years my one bathroom deserves honorable mention; now we have this beautiful office and a full bathroom. With a queen-size hide-a-bed, it can also be a guest room."

I could remember the quiet peace that enfolded us as Horace and Tennie, Harold and I prayed together, dedicating this office—and the bathroom—to God. That was seven years ago and now Harold was getting his view from Heaven. Today this place would be a refuge for our beloved pastor emeritus and his wife Tennie. Missionaries had stayed here, and my precious Jan and Jud enjoyed this hiding place during wonderful summers of sand, sea, and shrimp. The children stayed with me in the house.

Just a few short weeks ago everyone enjoyed the beach and returned home, refreshed. Then the beautiful rolling ocean turned into a raging sea with 20-foot waves and 115-mile-an-hour winds. Houses and piers washed to sea, and boats were hanging in trees.

Now—back to reality! Scrub the bathroom, make up the bed, clear the desk for Horace! I closed the door and prayed for God's peace to fill my beautiful office.

I thought of Larry Marbry, my young friend, the builder who had made this office possible—his gift to God and me. "God bless Larry 100-fold, Lord."

I remember reading that the glory of tomorrow is rooted in the drudgery of today. I chuckled to myself. "Must be lots of glory out there to match the endless washing and cooking; keeping peace with four dogs claiming territory and two cats who know how to hide; 12 people for showers and meals!"

I called Jeanelle. "We have power! Come for dinner—Horace and Tennie are coming."

Peter and Jeanelle came! Their home was spared, and power came on also—just trees down and much debris.

Horace and Tennie were not allowed back on the beach, and it took days before they could estimate the damage to their lovely home at Wrightsville Beach. The first-floor apartment was flooded, but their upstairs home was fine—even the pier stayed.

Chris barbecued chicken that Tennie had salvaged from her freezer, then we made five large blueberry cobblers from that rescue mission. Two were eaten at supper, then three put in the freezer for a Fran memorial day dinner.

While the wonder-working power of the dishwasher made background music, we gathered in the living room to hear Jeanelle play the great hymns of strength and comfort for the tomorrows ahead.

The night closed the door on this day. Come tomorrow, there would be a way.

The house was quiet. Katie was sleeping beside me, and I reached out to hold her. She snuggled in her sleep.

They were all here, under my roof—safe and asleep. Somehow I wondered if God from His view from the top was waiting for the day when His children would be Home—safe in His love.

"Oh, God, don't let anyone be missing."

I hugged Katie and fell asleep.

11

100 Mums

Sarah, I have had it with this hurricane mess—debris all over and limbs hanging over the broken fence."

Gus, the Shepherd, can find a way through stumps and branches, then comes around to be let in by the gate—a game he likes to play. Scout, the prissy Doberman, won't venture near the debris; she likes boundaries and stays in her place.

I can't remove the stumps, but I can certainly put some color in so I can see some beauty from my bay window. "Come on, Sarah! Let's go! On the corner of Wrightsville and College there are hundreds of mums, so let's get some of them." We were off!

"I like the rust color, but you pick out the ones that aren't in full bloom, with lots of buds." Sarah filled up the trunk with all colors, then we headed home to the garden shed and shovel.

We alternated colors and when we looked at the result of our work we saw rows of low mums—yellow, wine color, rust, and purple.

Sarah put a fence around the flowers to keep the dogs out of them. Gus just walked over the fence and found a quiet spot between the plants. So much for that protection! Scout walked away from the fence.

A young man told me that his generation had been put out to pasture without any fences. "If there had been fences I guess I would have jumped them, but then I'd have a fence to come back to."

Sarah was her grandfather's "Princess." To him she was a beautiful china doll to be protected. To Sarah, her "Papa" was a safe place—a fence to come back to.

At church she managed to squeeze in between us. "I'm coming between you," she giggled.

"For the Princess—there is room!"

Sunday dinner found her sitting beside Papa—even in her high-chair days. During games she looked up into the bleachers to be sure Papa was watching. He was!

They seemed to share secret jokes or search for forbidden candy in hiding places. They talked!

That was five years ago. Now we are planting mums to brighten up the drab landscape.

I looked over at the tall mums we planted after Harold's funeral. Five years ago Joyce, my sister, found me in the garage crying over his garden gloves.

"Come on—let's plant mums!"

We did! They are still blooming.

Now Sarah and I look from the bay window and see the beauty of color in the midst of all the debris.

Buddy, the yard man, is too busy to come and rake the yard. The fence men say "any day now." We wait while Gus slips through the hole.

The tree men didn't get back to grind up the roots—so we wait. "Well, Sarah, the mums look so great, let's go back and get more. We'll put them around the cul-de-sac at the end of the street."

"Grammy, that is really not necessary!"

"I know, but it is fun to drive up the street and see some life around here."

So the mums and periwinkles laugh together and defy the mess left by "Fran."

What does God see from His picture window? Does He see His children bloom where they are planted? Does He see faith coming through the debris from storms—a little color in a drab world? Does He see how much the "Princess" misses her "Papa"? Can her Papa see how she struggles to keep her balance in a culture without fences? Does he see her tears when she longs for his lap to curl up in and feel the protective fence of his loving arms?

If he were only here, I mused, he would understand the temptations that overtake our children. And what would he say? I can almost hear what he would say.

"Don't be afraid; she is planted in good soil, watered with love and prayer, and will grow in God's 'Sonshine.' Trust God!"

"Grammy, do you realize that we have planted 100 mums?"

"That's a good number, and I can't help but think how Papa enjoyed watching plants grow." *Watching you grow, too, Sarah,* I thought to myself.

"Look, Sarah, I bought *The Name Book* by Dorothea Austin, so let's look up your name."

Sarah: Princess; noble lady; beloved one.

"Ye shall have a song as in the night
When a holy solemnity is kept;
And gladness of heart,
As when one goeth with a pipe
To come into the mountain of the Lord
To the mighty One of Israel." (Isaiah 30:29)

Elizabeth: Oath of God; consecrated one.

"The gift of God is eternal life
Through Jesus Christ our Lord." (Romans 6:23)

"You also have a third name—Nightingale—since your grandfather Fisher was a descendant of Florence Nightingale. This elegant lady, who came from a wealthy home, had a 'call from Heaven' to care for the sick. For years her parents kept her busy with travel and an active social life, hoping to discourage her dream.

"Finally, at age 32, she persuaded her parents to allow her to pursue her dream—to nurse and to train others.

"During World War II it was Winston Churchill who reminded the world how 'so many owe so much to so few.' Since I am a nurse, I realize how much we owe to the pioneers in medicine.

"Do you realize, Sarah, that the principles your ancestor laid down have never been improved upon? God's laws can't be improved either. 'For ever, O Lord, thy Word is settled in heaven.' One judge told me it takes a million laws to enforce the Ten Commandments! To think we have people who want to remove those God-given laws!

"I wonder what Florence Nightingale would say about the millions of babies who never had a chance at life?

"What a beautiful name you have—Sarah Elizabeth Nightingale Jensen! You are indeed Papa's Princess, a noble lady and a beloved one—consecrated to God before you were ever born. You also have all the God-given creativity within you to make a difference in the culture that serves lesser gods.

"Well, Sarah, I must say we have done enough planting for one day—100 mums! Just think how beautiful they will look next year, and by that time all the debris from Hurricane Fran will be a memory.

"Let's go to Jackson's for a barbecue."

One hundred mums! Wow!

12

The Angel on a Tractor

I think you booked this luncheon too close to our Greensboro trip."

"Oh, I know, Chris, but I promised to go to a community luncheon about a year ago, and I must keep that engagement—not always easy to build a bridge of racial harmony in a rural area."

"Since the Methodist Conference in Danville, Virginia won't end until Tuesday night, you really should fly out of Greensboro rather than Wilmington on Wednesday."

"Oh dear, that means another suitcase. It's cold in Virginia, warm in Texas."

"Okay, Mom. Just go to your luncheon and I'll be here so we can leave as soon as you return. We'll make it to Greensboro by 6 P.M.; your host will meet you and take you to your conference; then I'll go with my friend Peggy to our meeting."

I hung up the phone. Chris was right! I did it again! Too-close connections! I missed Harold, who could manage details while I saw the overall picture. We made a good team!

All the bags and books for the Virginia conference were packed, and Chris would be here when I returned. I did remember to send books to Texas. Score one for my team!

We were to meet in Greensboro at the K & W cafeteria in Friendly Shopping Center. Now I was ready to go. With my car keys in hand and purse dangling, I headed for my car.

That was the moment Gus decided to find his escape tunnel, left by Hurricane Fran, to join other "escapees" in a run over at the college campus. I'm on the list for a fence repair, but somehow I have a feeling the old year will end without my number coming up.

What a sight I was running across campus: high heels, dressed for a luncheon, car keys and purse dangling, yelling, "Gus! Gus!"

Gus stopped, then, slowly dragging his tail behind him, came through the gate. I locked him in the garage!

With a deep sigh I managed to check my map and hit the road, over the river and Cape Fear Bridge.

Across the open fields the sun shone through fall colors, and with my memorized map of twists and turns I pulled into a gas station—just to be sure I was heading in the right direction.

"Keep right on going round the bend and over the railroad track. Just keep going—a long way!"

I kept going!

When I saw a farmer in the road I asked for the Methodist Church. Chewing on a wad of tobacco, he scratched his head thoughtfully. "Yes'm—right down yonder."

I went down yonder! An Episcopalian church!

I spotted a mother with young children in hand and I frantically waved my map. She drew her children indoors and shut the door. "No sales today!" was the message.

"Oh dear, I wish Chris was here. She can find any road."

Finally a child ventured through the door. "Please, honey, tell your mama I'm lost!"

The mother looked me over. "Can't miss it—big cemetery beside the church."

It was there! A Baptist church!

Now I had been over the railroad track three times. I was desperate.

Then I saw her! Waving my map I ran toward the woman on the tractor. "Please, I'm 30 minutes late—the *Methodist* church!"

"Follow me!" In a moment she was off the tractor, in her car—and I followed!

The hostess of the luncheon was scanning the roads for a sign of the speaker. As I ran into the church she beckoned the woman who'd helped me. "Come in! Come in!"

"Oh no, I can't go to a luncheon in my work clothes."

"Oh yes, you can! You brought our speaker!"

So it came to pass that we sat together at the community luncheon.

When I was introduced I said, "I've read of angels, heard of angels, but this is the first time I met an angel on a tractor." Laughter and applause erupted.

Before I told my stories, a choir of beautiful black children stood up to sing. A grandmother had gathered the children in her community to form a choir.

In their colorful outfits they swayed in rhythm to the grandmother at the piano and sang songs of joy in the Lord—in spite of difficulties. One little boy kept in step and knew the song. I wanted to reach out and hug him. I forgot all about the roundabout way over railroad tracks.

Once again I told the story of "the high-button shoes," one of life's most valuable lessons. With upturned faces the children laughed at the ugly shoes pulled from the missionary barrel.

"Those horrible button shoes were out—oxfords were in." The children nodded. I had them right in my heart.

"My Mama said, 'Pride is a terrible thing. Wear your shoes with a humble and thankful heart because it could be one of life's most valuable lessons. It is not so important what you have on the feet, but it is very important where the feet go.'

"But I didn't want valuable lessons—I wanted new oxfords."

My audience of young and old understood and nodded. I continued.

"My Mama taught these big lessons in a tiny house with an outhouse at the end of the path and a water tank in the kitchen. Today we have big houses and tiny lessons.

"My Papa didn't give me a choice. I had to wear those shoes, so big I had to put cotton in the toes. Mama said I had a choice how I would wear the shoes—with bitterness or a thankful heart."

As my gaze swept over the audience I said, "Life's barrel throws out its contents of broken dreams, broken hearts, and broken promises. Life is what happens to you while you are making other plans.

"Only God can take the broken things and make something beautiful out of our lives. We come to the cross and lay our burden down and ask Jesus to come into our lives. I was only six years old when I asked Jesus into my heart."

We sang together: "Jesus loves me, this I know, for the Bible tells me so."

After the luncheon, the children sang again. My angel on the tractor, with a tear on her cheek, slipped away to her car. I didn't know that life's barrel had thrown out broken dreams and hearts into her life. A husband had died, then she lost a son. Recently a grandson was murdered. I had read it in the paper but didn't know the name. Racial bitterness ran deep!

I marveled at the love of God, who reached everlasting arms across railroad tracks, open fields, and country roads to a time and place where a brokenhearted angel sat on a tractor.

Those loving arms of God brought her to hear not only the stories of hope and faith but to hear the black children sing of joy in the midst of sorrow.

I was "touched by an angel." My angel was touched by God.

P.S. Chris and I made it to Greensboro at the K & W—6:05 P.M.! I had a great conference at the First Methodist Church in Virginia. Now I'm on U.S. Air, winging my way to San Antonio, Texas. God's arm will reach there also.

13

The Week Before
Thanksgiving, 1996

I'm a little late, Grammy, but I stayed at the library to finish a paper."

"That's fine, Sarah. You are just in time to bake our Norwegian Christmas bread."

"Who did the tree?"

"Chad, Melissa, and Chris Rom [another Chris, heading for medical school] got the boxes out of the garage and decorated the tree while I put up my kitchen Christmas curtains and wreaths."

"You must be the only one to put up Christmas curtains and decorate before Thanksgiving."

"Guess I'm just a sentimental Grammy when it comes to Christmas. When I hear Bing Crosby sing, 'I'll be home for Christmas, you can count on me,' I just fall apart. I want to gather all my chicks under my wings and keep them safe from a new year of uncertain challenges. I know I can't do that. Only God can gather His children under

His wings, then strengthen them to travel an unchartered course.

"At least we can try and do what is in our power to do—and that is bake! The dough is all set and has been rising the last two or three hours."

"I'll scrub my hands and get a Christmas apron. Oh, you are too much—Christmas aprons, curtains, and Bing Crosby!"

"Divide the dough into five parts, then each one into three; roll in a long roll in cinnamon and sugar, then braid the three strands.

"That's the way! You'll be a good homemaker, Sarah—a creative touch.

"Look! Five loaves ready to stand in a warm place for another two to three hours—depends on how the dough rises. Since this bread baking is an all-day project, why don't you cook supper—just something simple while the dough rises?"

"Look, Grammy, here's a jar of spaghetti sauce, so I'll just cook spaghetti and we'll eat in the breakfast room."

"That's great! Your mom is picking up Katie, so we will be four since your father is working late into the night to finish a project before Thanksgiving."

It was time to put the bread in the oven.

I watched Sarah bustle around to set the table, then reached for frozen peas and applesauce. "I don't like plain peas, so why don't you make a cream sauce—the kind Papa and Uncle Howard always requested? "Come here and I'll show you how.

"Use real butter; stir the flour in the melted butter and slowly add milk to the right consistency; add salt, pepper and a little parsley for flavor."

"Wow! How will I ever learn when you don't measure anything—just a little of this and a little of that?" We laughed together.

"Can't you see me writing a cookbook? It would sound like Chinese!"

When Chris and Katie came they saw what Sarah was doing. Katie ran out to play with the dogs—not interested in cooking today.

"I'm hungry! Looks great, Sarah!"

"Dad's on the phone, Grammy. He's bringing his crew home for a quick supper, then back to work until morning."

"That means set the table in the dining room and mix the spaghetti sauce and noodles together—then *serve the plates!* I'll make a tray full of oven toast, and we'll add more creamed peas and applesauce. Don't worry—it will stretch!

"I remember the time your wonderful Papa brought seven preachers for lunch. I was scrubbing the kitchen floor in the Illinois parsonage. Gladys, my nursing classmate, was visiting me at the time and almost had a heart attack when she was introduced to seven preachers in the living room.

"I just finished the floor, washed up, brushed my hair, and put on a starched apron—just as I had watched my mother years ago. 'When unexpected guests arrive,' my mama said, 'just brush your hair and have a starched apron handy—then do what you have to do.'

"I did! My friend was frantic! 'What to fix?'

"This was Saturday noon, and I always cleaned first, then went to the store to get ready for Sunday. My mama used to say that the reason for Saturday was to get ready for Sunday. The house had to be clean, then the groceries for Sunday dinner had to be planned, followed by the Saturday night bath in the round tub beside the cookstove.

"One day someone came to the back door and Mama hid me and the tub under the table cloth. I nearly froze to death—the man wouldn't shut the door. Oh well, so much for that story!"

"Come on, Grammy, finish the story! What did you do?"

"I just rolled out biscuits and put one pan after the other in the oven. My poor friend was frozen in time! 'Come on, Gladys—just set the table. Believe me, we'll make it.'

"I got out the butter and my homemade strawberry jam and opened three jars of my canned Michigan peaches.

"The men devoured tray after tray of hot biscuits and coffee. The peaches were dessert. 'My wife would kill me if I did this,' one of the preachers said. Guess what your wonderful Papa said!

"'Why?'

"Everyone burst out laughing—everyone, that is, except my friend, who was going to tell Harold 'why' in no uncertain terms.

"So you see, Sarah, that life is what happens to you while you are making other plans. I never realized how much I learned from watching my mama years ago.

"Now you can remember what your great-grand-mother would say. 'Sarah, brush your hair and put on a starched apron! Then do what you have to do!'

"Shawn and Eric used to hide her slippers under the bed, then race to hunt for them. She would end up telling them a story and singing a Norwegian song. How you would have loved her.

"When Katie was small she used to say, 'I'd like to go to Heaven and sit on Bestemor's [Great-Grandmother] lap and hear her tell stories to the children in Heaven.'

"Sarah, sometimes I feel closer to Heaven than earth. Perhaps that is why I see things differently—my view from the top."

"Here they come!"

"Katie, pour the tea while Sarah serves the plates. Here's the bowl of creamed peas and the applesauce. Oh—some small side dishes for your Dad—he doesn't like food mixed. The toast is buttered, so we are ready."

We planned for four, but eight heads were bowed in prayer for God's blessing on the food.

He did! Everyone had enough and apple pie and Christmas cookies for dessert. The cars pulled out of the driveway—back to work until 4 A.M., to finish before Thanksgiving.

We wrapped the loaves of Yule bread, ready for gifts to family and friends. I had many more loaves to bake before Christmas.

Katie had to babysit, so Sarah and I cleaned up the kitchen. Bing Crosby was singing "I'm dreaming of a white Christmas." I was dreaming of a nice bed. It had been a long day.

Now it was Sarah's turn to leave. "Good night, Grammy. I love you."

"I love you, too, Papa's 'Princess' and 'my little cook.'"

P.S. Sarah is coming back. We have to pack a box of Yule bread for Janice and for Heather and Matt's first Christmas.

14

The Presents

Grammy, I don't have money for Christmas presents. What can I do?"

"You are creative, Sarah, so I suggest we jump in the car and get Christmas material, and you can make gifts. I'll show you how to do it."

Not bad! Christmas fabric was one-half price! With pillows, thread, and beautiful material, including gold tassels, we headed for home, where we used the breakfast table to cut out table runners, covers for pillows, and shoulder bags.

"I'll get my portable sewing machine."

"That's fine, and we'll set up the office for sewing, and I'll bring the old ironing board—the one Aunt Jan said, 'Get rid of it—shakes all over!' When Aunt Joyce came she marched me to Wal-Mart to get a decent ironing board, so I just put this old one in the garage." Now we were in business.

I almost suggested that Sarah could use my sewing machine, but then I remembered how Papa bought the portable machine for Sarah's birthday. A special gift for his "Princess" before he died. It was a day when Sarah was in a cheerleading competition on the University campus grounds.

"Come on, Margaret, let's go!"

"Harold, you can't go—too sick to be outside in this wind."

"You don't think I would miss the competition."

Later, when I looked around at the spectators, I realized we were the only white-headed grandparents in the crowd. Now and then Papa and Sarah's eyes met. She beamed!

When it was over, pictures taken, and congratulations in order, Katie slipped up beside her Papa. "Were you thinking of taking us to Swensons, Papa?" (That was the well-known soup, sandwich, and ice-cream place.)

"Come to think of it, I was thinking of just that, but I need to get back to bed. Here's the money—you take them out and I'll go home to bed."

Years later I heard Sarah say, "My Papa was so sick, but he came anyhow."

Not all gifts are as tangible as a machine; he gave other gifts to his grandchildren. A gift wrapped in love, not ribbons or tissue paper.

Sarah has a framed picture of her in her cheerleading outfit, sitting on Papa's lap, and both are laughing. That's how it was with those two—the "Princess and Papa."

While I was baking in the kitchen, Sarah made the gifts in my office. There was a pillow for Nanny (Grandma Fisher); a table runner with gold tassels and twelve napkins for her mother; a pillow and table runner for me; shoulder bags for Katie and friends.

There was one pillow left, and I wondered where it would go.

"I'm going over to see Aunt Mary [a family friend] and give her this gift."

It wasn't just a Christmas pillow. I knew it was Sarah's way of saying, "You've had a tough year—two surgeries and missing our family get-togethers—and I just want you to know I love you."

I'm sure she didn't say all those words—just smiled and said, "I love you."

Maybe Sarah's year hadn't been all that great—secret disappointments that we didn't know—and somehow she gave a gift of understanding without the tinsel and tissue of words.

Aunt Mary understood the true gift.

Somehow Christmas and gifts go together. Perhaps we say through gifts what we missed with words throughout the year.

I don't know why I'm crying again—just know how much I miss Harold at Christmas. I feel so silly crying while I'm baking cookies, just because I remember a pink sweater he gave me when I was 18 years old.

All my life I wore hand-me-down clothes, and when I opened up the package there was a beautiful pink sweater, with a dollar bill in the pocket. Now, I seldom had a nickel to spare while in nurses' training, and that dollar bill was like a bank to me. To think that was 63 years ago, and I'm standing in this kitchen wiping my eyes with a sticky apron.

"Please, Jesus, tell him 'thank you' for me; that after 63 years I still remember the sweater, and I'm not too sure I said 'thank you' often enough. Please, Jesus say 'thank you' for me."

From my view from the top of the years I think I shed more tears over what I didn't do than what I did wrong. Somehow it is easier to feel forgiven for mistakes that were made, but it is difficult to feel forgiven for the times I didn't show genuine thanks for small or big deeds.

How fast the years go! It seems like yesterday when Jan came home from Wheaton College with beautiful gifts for each one—Dan, Ralph, Harold, and me. She had worked nights in the Chicago post office to make the extra money. What a gift of love!

In the background I can hear the music of "I'll Be Home for Christmas," and I can still feel the thrill of Dan's Christmas with us after the year in Vietnam. I'll never hear the haunting tune without a longing to have Dan and Virginia for Christmas with all the family.

In the middle of watching the cookies and Sarah sewing in the office, the door suddenly opens, and I hide the tears in a sticky apron and put on a big smile. There stands Eric, grandson number three, in cowboy hat and boots—all six feet, six inches of him.

Long arms reach around the sticky apron, and I'm lost in the long arms of love. Eric is home for Christmas.

God has the most wonderful way of filling up the holes of longing for someone missing with loving for the ones near—God's gift.

The time of cookies and aprons with flour and sugar, sewing and cutting, Christmas bread and presents was over. Now the gift of Christmas Eve dinner with Ralph and Chris, then all off to the Christmas candlelight service where our beloved pastor emeritus Horace Hilton once more told the story of God's gift to the world.

We held our candles high—Eric (a little higher than the rest), Shawn, Ralph, Chris, Sarah, and Katie—and there I was having a problem again. I had trouble holding up my candle, a symbol of Jesus, the light of the world—those stupid tears started again. It's hard to hold a candle, cry, and blow your nose at the same time.

I did!

The tears were "Joy to the world, the Lord is come," God's gift to us.

15

The Fallen Oak

"No way I can tackle that tree, ma'am. Roots too big for any grinder around here." The mighty oak had crashed across other trees, but the hole from the uprooted roots was enormous.

"Grammy, I'll move the fence inside that tree, and we'll have to leave the tree and the tree house in the woods. Not a pleasant sight, but no one will touch it until the emergency restoration is complete."

Chad moved the fence, but the tree stayed crashed against smaller trees that were destroyed when the mighty oak fell in the hurricane storm. I'll have to plant roses along the fence to cover the background of fallen debris.

Nothing will be the same! It never is when trees of righteousness—God's mighty oaks—crash. The younger trees get caught in the downfall. I thought of Vance Havner's message, "Let me go Home before dark." I hummed a song from a long ago time: "Beneath the cross of Jesus, I would take my stand."

I couldn't help but remember the time Harold took us to a church dedication service up in the mountains of North Carolina. "Homecoming on the grounds" was the order of the day and we could almost taste the country ham, sweet potato pie, coconut cake, and pecan pie. There would also be the turnip greens, black-eyed peas, and hot biscuits.

The choir was in great form that day and dedicated the next number "to the Jensen family—our special guests." The choir sang with all the gusto of boundless joy: "Keep me safe in the hollow of Your hand; keep me safe till the storm passes by." They sang of the roll of thunder and the fury of the wind, but with a triumphant sound came "Keep me safe till the storm passes by."

I felt the tears come, and somehow I was lifted up into the safety of His arms.

I had come through some storms, and it must have shown because the choir leader said, "We'll sing that song one more time for Margaret Jensen." They sang it three times!

I looked at my fallen oak and thought of all the times I almost crashed in the storm—and then God drew me close to Him and held me until the storm passed by.

The fence was up, and the dogs were kept in a safe place.

Chris and I sat at the breakfast table this morning and talked about some storms—and some fallen oaks.

"Look, Mom, these Bible characters are so relevant to this day." She went to the bookshelf and reached for a Bible. "Our young people have a tough time in the hostile culture of today's cynicism against God, but do you realize how young some leaders were in the Old Testament?

"Amaziah—now who knows much about Amaziah? He was only 25 years old when he became king and reigned in Jerusalem for 29 years. The sad part was that he did right—but only partially. When he gathered his army he paid a fortune to recruit others—then he was stopped! A man of God said, 'Hey, you did the wrong thing recruiting other help, because God is not with them.'

"'What about all this money I invested in this venture?'

"The man of God answered, 'The Lord can give you much more that that.'

"He won the battle, then failed another test when he sought counsel from other gods. Then he died—a fallen oak through partial disobedience."

Chris and I made another pot of coffee.

It was quiet this Saturday morning. Our guests left for Greensboro, and we were alone—a special time to reflect over a past year of storms and battles.

The names were different, but the challenges are always the same: obedience to God's rules or turning to lesser gods.

One of our guests had asked if I ever felt guilty over the past. "Yes, I can look back with a perspective closer to Home than earth and see that what I thought was so important wasn't all that great."

I guess my "giving" nature got in the way of walking the tightrope of obedience to God. I was too quick to "help" in situations where angels feared to tread. It takes obedience to God to say "no"—even when it hurts.

Chris poured another cup of hot coffee; the other got cold while we were talking. "King Uzziah was only 16 years old when he took the place of his father, King Amaziah."

"Can you imagine our fun-loving Katie ruling a nation at 16?"

"She'd have everyone playing games and eating pizza."

"But listen to this! King Uzziah sought God and was instructed in the fear of the Lord. This is the bottom line! *As long as he sought the Lord, God gave him success.* He was a great king! He built towers, dug cisterns in the desert; he had vineyards and livestock, for he loved the soil. He made great machines for a powerful army, and his fame spread around the world."

"You know, Chris, the more we read the stories in the Bible, the more we see human nature is the same."

"I know. Here was this young king who became world famous. Then he crashed! When he became powerful the subtle enemy of pride destroyed him, and he was unfaithful to God. He died alone, separated from everyone because he had leprosy. He was even excluded from the temple.

"A mighty oak had fallen!"

Pride destroyed a great king. Humility and repentance restored King David. God is always ready to forgive and cleanse us from all unrighteousness.

Pride, bitterness, and unforgiveness have caused many powerful oaks to crash in the forest of humanity.

The coffee got cold again. We had much to think about.

When Chris left to go to the grocery store—for life goes on—I put the coffee cup down and went to my office to write.

The song from Sunday school came again and again:

I would be true
For there are those who trust me.
I would be pure
For there are those who care
       —*Hymn, "I Would Be True"*

Oh Lord, even when I'm old and gray, Don't forsake me;

Keep me close in the hollow of Your hand And let me stand, not fall, while the storm passes by.

16

Faith Lights

I watched the sun come through the white clouds with colors an artist would like to put on canvas. Billowing clouds covered the earth below like a soft down comforter, then dark clouds seemed to slip from behind the rim of nowhere.

"Fasten your seat belts—turbulence ahead!"

Below the world of clouds was another world of mountains, lakes, wheat fields, deserts, oceans with sandy beaches. There are days in that world when the dawn comes up like thunder with a splash of brilliant colors; then the dawn slips away to give the sun the right to rule the day.

When evening comes the sun leaves in a blaze of glory to allow the shadows to usher in the blanket of night and a million stars. God's picture-book!

In my imagination I look down through the clouds, now dark, while evening shadows slip into place. From my airplane view there are only clouds, with no visible world below, but I know there is a real world.

I come from that place of traffic jams, gangs and violence, angry motorists driving to the beat of defiant music, crowded airports, delays, lost luggage—all below the soft serenity of billowing clouds.

Within that world there is another culture of broken people huddled in shelters of peer pressure, iron bars, or homeless shelters—made by choices that brought chains instead of freedom. Deep within, beyond the hollow eyes, there is a child crying for someone to show the way to go home—home to a safe place.

I remember watching a bag lady push her cart of "collectibles," and I thought about the fact that she was someone's innocent baby, long years ago. What made her choose this road?

Across the street I saw a homeless man in coat and boots, too big, shuffle into the Salvation Army. In Sioux City, South Dakota, I watched as a homeless family was given a place of shelter and warm food on a cold night.

It wasn't always so!

In the beginning God made a perfect world and breathed His spirit into His creation, Adam and Eve, and all living things lived in harmony with God. A choice was made to rebel against God's perfect way, then down through the corridors of time, kings and kingdoms have made that same choice.

But God's love never changed!

Giants of faith line the hallway of faith where ordinary people lived extraordinary lives through the choice to obey God's rules.

Kings and kingdoms have passed away, but the "mountain people" stand like the Alps, undaunted by winds of changing cultures. For centuries the "faith people" believed that one day there would come the Messiah.

An old priest, worn with years of living, recognized the gift of God to the world, wrapped in a baby blanket. Simeon cried, "Now I can go Home; I have seen the Messiah."

Later the mob cried, "Crucify Him," but the disciples saw the risen Christ.

Today we also choose—to believe or not to believe. That choice affects everything we do.

My plane is above the clouds, beautiful soft clouds with some threatening shadows slipping into the magic moment.

"Fasten your seat belts—turbulence ahead!"

When Katie was small I used to tell her that when we get to Heaven we would slide down clouds and jump from one to the other. She believed in our wonderful make-believe world.

I settled back in my seat and continued to reflect on the miracle of faith. Somehow I felt safe, sheltered in God's love; somewhere beyond this earthly kingdom was my real Home.

The great heroes of the Bible marched before me, yet somehow I couldn't help but think of the "faith people" I have met in this life. We live in a kingdom within a kingdom and try to follow God's rules—an invisible kingdom of the heart.

In my memory I see the hollowed eyes of a generation of nonbelievers, showing their defiance in dress, hair, and music, "hanging out" on a corner. One day I watched a group of the same generation, with backpacks, off to a Third World country to build a school. A choice was made!

I thought of the bag lady with her collectibles in a cart and remembered a grandmother who took in crack babies to love. The kingdom of the heart within this world's kingdom.

The old man shuffling to the Salvation Army shelter made a choice someplace in life. In church last Sunday I watched a teenager with her head on her grandfather's shoulder. He made a choice!

I couldn't help but think of letters I get from prisoners who have been set free in the "heart kingdom" in spite of iron bars. "For God so loved the world, that he gave his only begotten Son, that whosoever believeth in him . . . should have everlasting life."

We come to God like children, with a simple faith to believe Him.

Across the pages of history we read of great "faith heroes" who blaze trails into the darkness of an unbelieving world: hospitals, schools, churches stand in the jungle of human misery.

Then there are the people who don't make headlines. In my mind and heart I see grandparents who opened the door one winter night.

"May we come home?" A father, with his children, came out of the storm of life to the safe place he knew—home!

Unconditional love enveloped the broken family until the day came when they became whole again. God's love in the marketplace!

I heard of a Russian wife who believed God within a kingdom of unbelief and prayed for her unbelieving husband for 30 years. One day his heart and eyes were open to the truth that God so loved him—and he believed.

Across the miles I met a grandfather who quietly teaches the Bible to his grandchildren.

One Christmas season I was a guest in a home where Mr. and Mrs. Santa Claus (not really!) opened their Christmas house to children, then gave gifts to remind them of God's gift to the world, Jesus.

While young people from earth's kingdom strive for identity and meaning, a newlywed couple fly to South Africa to give themselves in service in a hospital of broken bodies.

God's rules are different from our man-made rules: "Lose yourself and then find meaning."

I didn't feel like reading—just remembered sights and sounds of a world below the clouds.

Sometimes I wonder how God sees the "ordinary us," living out our faith in the marketplace of everyday living. Perhaps He sees us as "faith lights" of earth penetrating the darkness to show the light of the world, Jesus.

The "faith lights" bring hope in despair, joy in sorrow, peace in turmoil, love instead of hate, that kingdom within a kingdom—God's "faith lights."

P.S. I see the lights of the runway. Time to land. Home, Wilmington, North Carolina. All over the world the "faith lights" keep shining.

17

The Recipe Book

I think you should write a cookbook, Margaret, because when I read your books I put on the coffeepot and think of food." The caller urged me to give out some recipes, and I chuckled over the phone, just thinking about it.

"Guess what, Katie? Someone wants my recipes."

"That would be a disaster! Just ask my mom—a little of this or that, a pinch of this or that—like Chinese."

"Never mind, young lady, I can still teach you a thing or two. Your Bestemor was an excellent cook, but you should see her recipe book! Very hard to read or follow!

"Believe me, her recipe for life wasn't hard to read, and she began teaching us the value of discipline in everyday living when we were very young.

"Your Bestemor believed there were more discipline disabilities than learning disabilities. There is something freeing in the routine of the ordinary. She believed in doing with all your might what you had in your hand.

"When I was six years old she put me on a stool and taught me how to wash dishes. 'Wash, rinse, dry, and put away. Never leave dishes in the sink!'

"Then she took me by the hand and taught me how to make a bed. 'Never leave a bed not made!'

"She taught me how to set a table, and she always had a starched table cloth, even if made out of feed sacks, and different embroidered napkins for each one of us. We sat together, and no one left the table until all were finished—and then thanked Mama for the meal.

"In our culture today we have lost social skills because of our frantic schedules. We need to learn them again. Around the table we learned from each other, and our guests and our lives were enriched.

"When Aunt Jan was six years old I taught her the same way and she taught Heather. As the president's wife at Gordon College, Jan has made Wilson House a beautiful memory for guests. Her creativity comes through as she studies gourmet and table-arranging books, all to make a lovely setting for guests to enjoy.

"When I was visiting we went to a farm to get fresh flowers for her table. Believe me, she won't have a wrinkle on the table cloth. I know, since I ironed it over again. She just laughed and said, 'Who taught me?' What could I do?

"'Mom, I couldn't do all the entertaining, from picnics to formal dinners, if I hadn't learned the discipline of the ordinary day that gives freedom to think and plan.'

"So Katie, you never know what the future holds for you, so now is the time to learn from your mother.

"Routine is a blessing because you don't have to think about making a bed—just do it. That goes for laundry or dishes; just do them without thinking and that relieves much stress. Thinking about our duties is more stressful than just doing them.

"You'll seldom find an unmade bed or clutter in all your aunt's homes—or mine—because we were so used to Mama's recipe: 'Make bed, hang up, put away in its place.' Just that simple recipe for order takes away stress.

"Now my father was strict, and his recipe was 'Obey, respect, stand up straight, look people in the eye, and speak up!' He also had a 'thing' about 'Polish your shoes!'

"Believe me, that saves many arguments. Just do it!

"During one of my speaking trips I met an unusual family, a father and beautiful mother of ten children. She home-schooled her children, and the eldest was leaving for college. She was upset at the rude manners of many teenagers and decided to include a course in social graces in her teaching. It must have been hilarious, because she had them practice on each other.

"The boys seated their sisters at the table. (No, Katie, they didn't pull the chair *away*—maybe thought about it! The more I think about that, it would make a good home video, especially when introducing each other.) Poor Mom wasn't so sure it was working because they turned it into high drama. But one day she saw that it worked.

"A guest came to visit, and the mother said, 'Mrs. Smith, this is Johnny, and Johnny, meet Mrs. Smith.'

"Poor Johnny hung his head shyly and almost hid behind his mother, when suddenly a light went on and he reached out his little hand and said, 'I'm pleased to meet you.' He stood straight and tall!

"At the table she taught them how to place a napkin in the lap, what silver to use, not to leave the table unless excused, and always to say, 'Thank you for the lovely dinner.'

"This mother was beautiful—looked like a college girl—and told how difficult it was to keep the discipline in order, but when they were invited someplace socially she noticed that the social graces were in place. In spite of all the fun and drama, they were learning.

"The boys knew that honking the horn in the driveway was 'out' but coming to the door was 'in.' 'I am Johnny Smith—and when do you want Mary home?'

"Well, Katie, you've had quite a story, but good manners make everyone comfortable. I remember when Uncle Jack would come, and we could hear him tapping his cane. You would get the boys upset because you said, 'Stand up, boys, and shake hands. Uncle Jack is coming, so mind your manners.'

"'There goes Miss Bossy!' they'd say. But they did it!

"Uncle Jack grew up with gracious manners and expected the same from the children. He was 87 years old when he went Home—his view from the top.

"I remember thinking that he couldn't identify with young people since he never married or had a family. At his funeral we were all amazed at how many young people said he had been their role model. 'He was always there, in his place in church, faithful and ready to encourage us to finish school, make good grades—and remind us to read Proverbs.' For birthdays or graduation he gave copies of *My Utmost for His Highest* by Oswald Chambers.

"Like his brothers Howard and Harold, he was a Southern gentleman."

It was time for Katie to go home, but we would find time to share stories again, probably over ice cream at Swensons.

The settings might change, but truth is eternal and the old remains new. The fads of today grow old by tomorrow.

It is quiet now. I could talk to Scout, but he's asleep, not in a listening mood. Perhaps I'll make a cup of tea and read a book.

Out of a folder slipped a clipping from the Wilmington *Star-News*. It was a story about a woman from New York, Anny, who received a package from her mother. She was stunned, because her mother had died in a Jewish concentration camp. In the package was a crumbling, hand-stitched book containing recipes from her mother and other women of the camp.

The recipes must have fed their souls with memories of preparing food and sharing with guests at a table with white linen, beautiful china, and silver.

I put my tea cup away. Somehow I could see these starving women in rags, perhaps with lice and bugs as guests, huddled together sharing their recipes—the ones they dreamed of giving to their daughters. Their memories had stored up the cinnamon, strudels, and dumplings while their numb fingers wrote the words.

Fifty years later the cookbook, *In Memory's Kitchen*, a legacy from the women of Terezin, became a centerpiece at a luncheon put on by the United States Holocaust Memorial Museum. The book had gone from hand to hand, from Auschwitz to the Drake's Gold Coast room in Chicago.

The mother's chocolate cake was served by waiters in white coats.

On my shelf was a book called *The Hiding Place*. For hiding the Jews in their Holland home, the Ten Boom family died in the Auschwitz concentration camp. Corrie ten Boom was the lone survivor who later traveled around the world to tell of the depth of God's love.

Through the story I could visualize the gaunt women in the lice-infested barracks of Auschwitz huddled over a book—a recipe for eternal life. From the dark pit of evil and death they fed on the living bread and water of life.

Someday, the Living Word will host the table with Heaven's splendor.

With open arms He still invites all to "come and dine."

18

Today, I Cry for Me

Into every life there comes a time when we feel like a 'nothing scroonched-up ball'—and crawl under a table and just 'cry for me.'" Lena, my heart friend, a symphony in black, poured a cup of coffee. A faraway look slipped across her face, like a shadow from a long-ago time.

She continued. "When I was young I worked in New York, and one day my fine white lady gave the menu for dinner—and a pound cake for dessert. I had never made a pound cake!

"Out of fear I just crawled under the dining room table like a 'nothing scroonched-up ball' and cried. 'Jesus, Jesus, I be Your child. Don't let Your black child be put to shame. Teach me to bake a pound cake.' Your Word says 'I will instruct and teach you' so I cry, 'Teach me!'

"He did!" With a chuckle she added, "And now I be called the 'queen of pound cakes.'"

That was 25 years ago when I heard the story. Now Lena's pound cakes are history, but she left a legacy of childlike faith when she went Home.

There have been times when I have curled up in Harold's leather chair and felt like a "nothing scroonched-up ball"—and just cried for me.

Most of the time I abound with the joy of living and praise God for the challenges of open doors for service. The love and prayers of the family of God enfold me like a warm comforter. When U.S. Air lands in Wilmington, loving arms are there to bring me home.

Alone in the quiet house, with bags unpacked, I curl up in the empty leather chair and that "nothing scroonched-up ball" feeling comes—and I cry for me.

That's when I remember the empty places in the family, and not only empty places but empty hearts in those dear to me. When I am bursting with the mercy and grace of God, the overflowing love from beautiful people across the miles—then why cry for me?

I cry because I think I have given all there is to give— my love, my strength, pleading prayer—and still across the miles there are empty places in the hearts of those dear to me. Where did I fail?

I seem to hear Lena. Could it be from her view from the top? "We all gets there, child—but then we gets up and bakes a cake. Just let God fill the empty hearts, but fill your own with praise."

In my mind I brought a Bible story of long ago into a setting of today; not the King James version, but close enough! I could visualize a Jewish mother curled up in a "nothing scroonched-up ball"—crying for herself. Despair was draped around her shoulders like a heavy mantle.

Someone drew near and tapped her on the shoulder. "What are you doing?"

"I'm crying for me! Events have happened so fast, and I have been too numb to cry, but now it is all over—and I'm crying for me."

"What do you have in your house?"

"What do I have? Such a question! Two good eyes can see there is nothing!"

"What do you have?"

"Mr. Prophet Man, do you know what Empty Empty means? Empty is when furniture is gone from the house—empty! Empty Empty is when hope is gone from the heart. Empty Empty! My Jake was a good man; went to school to study the ways of God. Then he died! Have you noticed, Mr. Prophet Man, how good men die and the wicked live?

"I could tell you things about wicked men who prosper—a butcher cheats on chickens, and the man with the secondhand store who took my furniture cheats widows. I know! Oye! The bills! Yesterday I sold Jake's books and desk. Oh, such a good man, my Jake.

"See my boys over there on the swing? Jakey is like his father, but Sammy, the youngest is like me—good-looking, eh?

"The house—you still asking what is in the house? Look! Look—see for yourself. Empty! Empty!

"That's not all, Mr. Prophet Man. Tomorrow they come for my boys—to pay off debts. Do you know what could happen to two nice Jewish boys in this world of wicked men? Such a world where good men die and the wicked live? So, you keep asking—so look!

"This house used to be filled with books and music. Jake played with the boys while I mended socks. So good it was! Now—empty! Empty!

"How fast laughter can turn into mourning! Sometimes I hear the sounds of the past, like a haunting melody in a minor key.

"So! What is in the house? Come—we look! So? A bottle of olive oil? Take it! No good to me—not even a pot to put it in.

"What did you say? Go borrow from neighbors! The neighbors shared their last chicken with me. So now I ask for a pot? What's to cook?

"What? Go! Go! So, a fool I am already—a disgrace! Wait! I remember something Jake said. 'We fight the battle in the will.'

"You say, 'Go!' I say, 'Foolishness.' A battle! Ha, some things come back to me. Abraham: God said, 'Go!' He went! Moses: 'Go!' He went! Sometimes what we don't see is more real than what we see. Yes? So now you say, 'Go! Get the pots!'

"Jakey! Sammy! Come quick! Go to Aunt Chris, get the big shrimp pot; then to Aunt Mary for the soup kettle; run—to Aunt Beverly—the big one. Go! Go!

"So? Do I have time to explain? Don't ask! Go! You heard the Prophet Man, Jakey. Close the door and pour!

"Sammy, *we are in the oil business!* What? All the gas stations, Wal-Mart—all out of oil? We sell! Good price!

"Sammy, go pay the butcher what we owe! Jakey! Get the furniture back—and the bicycles, and count your Papa's books.

"Look! the lamps are lit! Stay for supper, Mr. Prophet Man—please. You like herring in wine sauce?

"Go, Jakey! The deli—*fresh* everything! No day-old bread!

"Oh, Mr. Prophet Man—not so empty the house? The table is set, the lamps are lit, and the glory of the Lord fills this house. Emmanuel, God with us, fills the heart.

"Sammy, Jakey—this man is the chancellor of the university, Dr. Elisha. Someday, maybe, Dr. Elisha, the boys could go to your school? They must learn that God's ways are not our ways. There is no explanation or understanding the works of God! Remember, Jakey and Sammy, we live by promises—not explanations."

P.S. I must remember to tell Katie my version of "Empty Empty. Today I cried for me—not for long. If you won't believe, then tomorrow I'll cry for you.

19

The Nine O'Clock

I closed my desk. It was time to pack for a 6:40 A.M. flight to Alabama. How a week of work can march into one day, I'll never understand. When interruptions leap into a planned schedule I seem to hear Eldred (all the way from Seattle) whisper in my ear, "Time for God's grace."

"Hey, Grammy, I'm on my way to Raleigh, and I need some pancakes to fuel my energy tank. Great year! Great opportunities out there!"

I flipped the pancakes—not one but three—with an egg in each one, then buttered and rolled in powdered sugar. "God's grace!" I heard it again.

Full of enthusiasm, Shawn, number-two grandson, was ready to change the world in 30 days or less. I could hear a tape recording in my mind playing all the wonderful messages I had stored for such a moment as this. This one I had rehearsed many times and had probably given it verbally, but with less results than seemed worthy of such wisdom. On the other hand, a good sermon bears repeating.

It doesn't seem fair that my flower garden and Scout, my faithful companion, should be the audience. To the wind I could say out loud, "Now, Shawn, it is always a good thing to finish what you begin.

"Even Paul the apostle says, 'This one thing I do,' and in my years of learning I have discovered it is good to do one thing at a time. Before I changed the world, Shawn, I would get my college degree behind me. Even if you don't go into that field of study, it is character building to finish, and I've never met anyone who regretted finishing—but I have witnessed regret over unfinished business.

"One of my classmates had three months to finish and ran off and got married. I met her later, with tears in her eyes and a broken marriage."

Then my tape recorder keeps going on—all the notes I had rehearsed. "Always seek God's will first, and the rest will follow."

Now I could write a chapter on wisdom. "Oh yes, Shawn—read Proverbs every day."

I must sit down and show Shawn the notes I had in my Bible; some Harold had written also. "Wisdom is the key to life, and the beauty and art of living is to have every area of our life under God's will." I guess that would go along with yoking up with God's will and learning of Him—not bearing life's burdens alone.

Why is it so hard to fear the Lord, when that is the beginning of wisdom? Oh dear, will I ever be able to tell them what I have learned in 80-plus years? Time goes so fast, and there is so much to tell.

To fear the Lord is to think of God with awe and reverence, walk in humility, and depend on our Creator. Why is that so difficult?

I must try to answer that because I have learned that the cares of this world and our secular culture have a powerful influence. The battle is fought in the will.

God says, "Come and learn." We would rather "run and do." We have to choose eternal values over the secular culture, and that is a battle.

Shawn kept talking on the phone and eating. My recorder kept clicking while I waited for my chance. *When he is full of pancakes he will be happy to listen to my sermons— maybe?*

I even thought of wise and prudent, wise and practical. Laundry, every week—prudent, and so is a clean room. I doubt if the "prudent" fits in with the great adventures of the New Year.

Then there was the day he said, "Grammy, I need to learn to keep a budget. Will you help me?" Would I help this brilliant child? With a notebook and pen and simple instructions I started him on the road to becoming a world accountant.

I think the hurricane got that notebook—never been found.

Then there's that cap on Shawn's head! Oh well, the cap and lessons on manners can wait. Enough already! Now is my chance!

Shawn finally finished eating and stopped talking on the phone. "It's Aunt Jan, Grammy!"

"Mom, just to remind you about the nine o'clock—call me back when you are alone."

"Leaving, Shawn? Just a minute. I'll just pray for you before you leave."

"Jesus, Shawn is your precious child, and You will instruct him and teach him in the way he should go and guide him with Your eye. Thank You. Amen."

"Thanks, Grammy. By the way, I'll be back for Sunday dinner." The truck pulled out of my driveway. *No sermon!*

Better call Jan. "Don't forget the nine o'clock, Mom."

How could I forget? The nine o'clock is the agreement we made to "call out their names." It was Lena's call to prayer. "Child, call out the names before the Lord."

Sometimes the nine o'clock is just that—a phone call at 9 A.M., and Jan and I call out the names of our children—and other needs. At times it is 9 P.M. when Jeanelle and Peter call out the names. Today it was 4 A.M. In California it was 6 A.M. when Jan stopped at 9 A.M.

Wherever we are, at some time we join with Aunt Joyce, Aunt Grace, Chris, Jeanelle, and Peter, and invite others to join the nine o'clock. We come in the name of Jesus to make our requests known at the throne of God.

When I am alone I place a map before me and call out the names of family and friends, all around the world. With Peter's missionary heart he cries out for Africa—where his heart is. All over the world God's Spirit is at work as God's children "call out the names" of their families and friends.

Sometimes it seems too routine—over and over. Then there are times when God's Spirit puts a burden for a special need—and I'm awake at 3 A.M.

Across the miles I hear, "Mom, I've seen many answers this year, and I believe it is the nine o'clock."

When I looked back I cried out to God, "I can't see specific answers, but by faith I know You are at work."

Jan reminds me, "Sometimes we talk so much to our children they can't hear God—so let's pray and talk to God about our children instead." To think of all the good sermons I've had stored up in my mind recorder—just must remember the nine o'clock.

Once again I seemed to sense Lena's presence. "Now child, you be learning. Just pull up a chair across the table and talk to Jesus." I did just that! "Jesus, we need to talk."

That's how Lena used to do it. She didn't call it the nine o'clock; she called it the "stretching out time."

That is when she stretched out on a blanket under the high hospital beds in the infirmary and called out the names of students. "Jesus talked back and I got a verse; now I gets a beat and gets me a song."

I sat with the empty chair—but not really empty, because the presence of the Lord filled the kitchen. I started to sing!

Are you weary? (Yes, Lord, I get weary.)
Are you heavyhearted? (Oh yes, I get heavyhearted when the young don't walk in Your ways.)
Are you grieving over joy departed? (I miss Harold.)
Then tell it to Jesus.

I did!

"What a friend we have in Jesus. . . . What a privilege to carry everything to God in prayer."

P.S. Shawn, while your truck hit I-40 to Raleigh at 70 mph (I'm sure!), I thought of all I didn't get to tell you, so I did a better thing—I called out your name.

Jesus can tell you in His way.

I love you, Shawn.

20

Jeremiah

The wind whipped the cold rain against the umbrella while I ran to climb up the steps of the U.S. Air Express. Balancing the windblown umbrella in one hand while hanging on to my book bag in the other I promised myself, "Never will I do this again!"

I made it! The bumpy trip was like a "rock-a-bye baby lullaby," and I fell asleep.

A warm car was waiting for me at the end of the line, and I settled in to enjoy a 90-minute trip from the airport to a beautiful resort, Lakepoint State Park.

Since I had several hours before the dinner meeting I slipped into a deserted dining room for a cup of coffee and grilled cheese sandwich. Glass windows overlooked endless lakes and small islands where ducks seemed to enjoy the cold rain and gray skies.

Warmed by good coffee, I hurried to my room to unpack and perhaps work on my forthcoming book. Most of the time I don't pay attention to pictures in a hotel room since they seem alike to me. This time I did! From my desk I looked up into the face of Jeremiah.

No, not the prophet Jeremiah, but Jeremiah, the raccoon.

Since this resort area was famous for its wildlife, the pictures depicted the animals and birds in beautiful art form. Jeremiah! Those black eyes looked right at me, and I had to put my pen down to gaze at the life-size form of a lovely animal that took me back to a long-ago time.

Ralph, the prodigal, had come home from a far country, but his friends thought they should come to rescue him from his family. It didn't work! Too much prayer had surrounded the "rebels"—and they stayed! That is when Jeremiah came into the picture.

Handsome, blond, and blue-eyed Keith, with hollowed eyes that mirrored near destruction from drugs, walked into our home in his cutoff jeans and bare feet with a baby raccoon on his shoulder.

"Eeks!" I let out a scream. "A raccoon!"

Ralph, now changed by God's love, gently pulled me aside. "Mom, Keith thinks the only reason he has to live is to take care of this baby raccoon that he found beside its dead mother. Go along with it."

When dinner was served, there was Keith at the table feeding the raccoon with a doll bottle. I swallowed hard, but kept quiet. Ralph's warning eyes were on me!

When it was time for bed, the raccoon slept beside Keith.

There did come a time when I gave out a blood-curdling scream! The raccoon thought that my shoe was his private bathroom—a "raccoon potty." "Don't scream, Mom, you'll upset Keith!"

"Upset Keith! What about me?"

"Shhh! Mom, you can always get new shoes, but we can't replace Keith."

I got new shoes!

Jeremiah grew into a beautiful pet with a distinct personality of his own. During the hot summer when I worked in my garden I would suddenly feel cold little feet climbing up my bare legs; then he would jump on my shoulder.

"Jeremiah! Don't you frighten me like that. You really are a rascal! You know that, don't you?"

He turned his laughing black eyes on me and begged. Yes, he did! Raccoons talk, you know.

"Okay, what do you want this time?"

He jumped off my shoulder and ran to the large tin of marshmallows. He begged again in his chirping language.

"Okay, you can have one—but that's it!"

From the tin of marshmallows I handed one to this begging animal; then he ran to the creek for his afternoon snack.

He said "thank you" before he left. We understood each other.

Before I realized it he was back again, climbing up to my shoulder. I gave in! So one more won't hurt.

In the meantime, while Keith was watching over his raccoon, God was watching over his child who had wandered to a far country.

One day Keith, the prodigal, came back to God's house. His life was changed by the power of the gospel.

"For God so loved Keith, that He gave His only begotten Son." Keith believed!

Jeremiah grew up and headed for the woods and the running stream. In that romantic setting he met Mrs. Jeremiah, and they lived happily ever after.

Keith's life overflowed with God's love. Then one day he married a beautiful Southern girl.

The day came when God called Keith Home. His purpose had been fulfilled; to us it seemed too soon, but we don't understand God's eternal purposes.

Looking out over the gray lake with stormy clouds getting darker, I remembered a night of storm in Greensboro. A scratching sound at the kitchen door brought my attention, and I opened the door against the stormy wind.

A frightened dog, covered with wet mud, stood shivering in the rain. Within moments Ralph had the black and white dog bathed and beside the fireplace, wrapped in a blanket.

The dog refused to leave, even after the storm. Then weeks later he said goodbye, wagged his tail, and left his safe place.

Months later there were another storm and scratching sounds at the back door. There stood our wet dog holding a tiny kitten in his mouth.

Within minutes I had warm milk for the tiny kitten, rubbed him dry, and wrapped him in a washcloth. Then I placed him in a shoe box.

The dog, now dry and warm, just cocked his head and looked at me, then stood watch over the kitten.

"Well, I guess you must have remembered the last storm. Some dog you are!" He understood! He looked at the kitten, and with a "thank you," he left.

The kitten grew into a beautiful big tomcat and stayed many years. We never saw the dog again.

One day I picked up the paper and read about two young girls who had been abandoned by their mother and given shelter and food by a homeless man. With tears in his eyes he took the children to the police and said, "I can't do any more for these babies. Take care of them. I just love them like my own."

I sat for a long time looking at Jeremiah, those dark eyes looking right at me, and I could almost see him begging for a marshmallow. A lonely baby raccoon, two small abandoned children, a tiny kitten in a storm, and a lonely prodigal—all found a safe place.

When I closed my eyes I could almost hear Keith strumming his guitar and singing his favorite song (from his view from the top): "Great is Thy faithfulness, oh God, my Father."

P.S. If His eye is on the sparrow, don't you think He's watching over you?

21

The U-Haul

With the open garage doors and the truck backed to the entrance, Chad and his friends could load up the U-Haul with the "garage treasures." For the past year Chad had made the garage his home, but now he was on to new adventures. The downtown art studio had been stripped of his beautiful paintings and, now covered, they were placed carefully in the U-Haul.

The seascape was for me—two young boys (Chad and Shawn) playing in the sand. "Not finished, Grammy; little Eric has to be painted—and a boat in the distance. Sorry—can't have it yet."

It was beautiful, and I knew just the place for it. "Come on, let's fuel up your energy tank with pancakes; then you can accomplish more work." The painting with the two young boys in the sand brought back memories. More pancakes!

Chad said, "Melissa, you can't imagine what it was like when we were young kids. Grammy had a beat-up Datsun, with a board over the holes in the trunk. All our pails, shovels, and inner tubes were stored there. The air conditioning only worked in the winter, so all the windows were open—sand and wind blowing everywhere.

"We were six little kids and Grammy. With a red bandana and an old housecoat over her baggy bathing suit she put the 'pedal to the metal' and headed for the beach. To keep us quiet she told stories and made up songs. We all joined in:

> Sea gull, sea gull
> Up in the sky,
> We can see you
> Flying so high.
> Please, oh please
> Don't go away
> We'll come back
> Another day.

"We piled out of the car and Grammy did a number on the lifeguard. 'Please help me keep track of those six towheads—yes, one, two, three, four, five, six—three girls and three boys.'

"Grammy came in and splashed with us but usually had her rear to the waves—and then a big one would come and catch her while we ran to shore."

More pancakes!

"That's not all, Chad. I remember the day I went out for a swim, but the undertow was bad that day and I had trouble getting to shore. Little Shawn saw me and ran into the waves. 'I'll help you, I'll help you!'

"When I saw that little blond head running into the waves to 'rescue me,' I used every ounce of strength and made it—then grabbed him up in my arms. 'My brave hero!' Whew! That was a fright!"

"Well, Melissa, we had our fun, then full of sand we piled into the Datsun and headed for home—shower, lunch, *and a nap!*

"I hated naps! Grammy had a no-nonsense attitude about naps. Believe it or not, I fell asleep right away.

"Up from the nap; then milk and cookies. This time Papa called out, 'Okay, kids—back to the beach!'

"We watched Papa duck Grammy, but she managed to get back at him.

"You know something? Those memories are the greatest!"

I listened.

"But you know what? This year has been one of the best years of my life. I got to do everything I wanted to do—paint in my own art studio, teach art, meet incredible people in the arts, get good parts in winning plays, and now a great acting part in a movie to be shown on T.V.

"Besides all the hard work, endless rehearsals, script writing, commercials, and building and designing sets for plays, I even had time to do some great surfing.

"Besides, look how lucky Grammy was to have me—her number-one grandson!"

"That's it! Get back to work! I'll do the laundry and put a macaroni-and-cheese casserole in the oven."

"If only you could do seafood like Mary Ann!"

"That's enough from you, Chad!"

By the time the laundry was finished, the U-Haul was packed. Boxes were packed for storage in the garage, then the garage was swept clean. It looked so empty!

The crew managed to empty the macaroni-and-cheese dish, then got ready to leave.

They were quiet now. Change is not easy. Leaving a safe place for the unknown adventures in New York took courage—and a few tears.

I assured Chad that God will direct the steps of His children—also the stops—when we ask for His guidance.

The plan for the future was graduate school, but auditions and rehearsals were in the present for Chad.

These are the days for new challenges—when you are young—but it still is not easy to leave the familiar for new territory. With my arms around them I prayed for God's protection and guidance and a pleasant journey.

I watched the U-Haul disappear from my view—but not from God's.

I sat down with a cup of coffee, then wondered if I had told Chad what he needed to know. I thought about the times Chad and I drank hot cocoa with marshmallows, late at night, and told stories.

Melissa and other "adopted grandchildren" sat around our Sunday dinner table and heard some ridiculous stories that the children recalled.

By this time the U-Haul must be heading out to I-40, loaded with earthly treasures. What had I given Chad to remember as treasures of the heart? Somehow I couldn't think of any great wisdom that I had packed into the U-Haul of the soul. For some reason it seemed that I was always cooking and calling out, "Katie—mash the potatoes." While Sarah filled the glasses with tea, perhaps I should have filled up the soul with great eternal truths.

Then there would be "Clear the table, girls" or "Come on, Shawn, pour coffee—time for dessert." Over coffee and dessert—more jokes and stories; I couldn't seem to get in all the great eternal truths that should have been packed into the soul's U-Haul.

I wanted to tell Chad before he left to never lose sight of "the old rugged cross"; that on that cross Jesus reconciled man to God. I should have told him that "Calvary is the pivot upon which time and eternity turns."

Those great sayings don't come out right when you are pouring tea and everyone is laughing at a funny story.

Then there was the time that I wanted to take gentle Melissa in my arms and tell her how much God loves her (she probably knows that)—but that was the time the dogs got into an argument about a ball. That timing didn't seem right.

Sometimes our young people get hung up on religion, and I wanted to explain that it was not religion but a relationship with God through Jesus Christ, His Son.

I could picture the U-Haul filled with "treasures" and Chad filled with macaroni and cheese—but did I fill the soul's U-Haul with eternal treasures? Are the songs, stories, messages stored away to be remembered?

It seems to me, sitting here with my coffee cup, that there were untold truths that I should have shared—or were they told in between the pancakes or mashed potatoes and meatballs? That all seems so ordinary, when I long to tell about greatness.

Perhaps next time I'll remember to tell what I heard and stored in my soul's U-Haul. During an Easter message I remember hearing how all the political, military, and religious powers joined forces to kill one lonely Man. This Man stood alone—forsaken!

This was the Man who healed the sick, fed the crowd, forgave sin, traveled with fishermen, ate with sinners, cleansed lepers, and made the blind to see.

The frenzied crowd roared, "Crucify him!"

The military, political, and religious powers had joined forces! When Jesus cried, "It is finished," they did not understand. While the world was still and the guards asleep, quietly the stone rolled away.

I read that all the philosophers of the world are stopped at the open grave. Up from the grave He arose! God did it all alone!

Somehow it seemed to me that I had failed to give out these great messages that I had tucked away in my soul's U-Haul! Laughter, music, dogs barking, ice in glasses; "Katie! Mash the potatoes!" Chris calling, "Get to the table! Last call!" For a quiet moment we joined hands and Ralph asked a *short* blessing.

"Remember the time Uncle Jack slapped Nanny's hand when she reached out to join hands for the blessing?" (He thought she was "fresh"—both were 85.) With everyone laughing I really couldn't expound on anything profound.

After dessert there was a game to watch, while Chris and I went into our routine. "Katie, Sarah—clear the table. Shawn—rinse. I'll load the dishwasher." I put the food away—believe me, not much—then, "Take the garbage out, Chad."

Whew! Kitchen clean!

Chris and I poured another cup of coffee and read the paper. "I've had it—can't read anymore. I'm off for my nap!"

"Me, too, Chris. I'm taking the phone off the hook, and we'll have an hour's peace and quiet."

I could hear them all laughing—probably telling jokes on me. I fell asleep!

When evening came and I was alone I opened Harold's Bible. "Blessed is the people that know the joyful sound: they shall walk, O Lord, in the light of thy countenance" (Psalm 89:15).

Then I opened a devotional by C. H. Spurgeon, titled *Morning and Evening*. "Mighty to Save" (Isaiah 63:1) was the heading: "God is mighty to save—to give new hearts, to work forth in them, to bend the knee before Him; mighty to finish the work He started. God is mighty to carry on His work in you—or to begin in others."

I remember Lena saying, "This house be a house of joy—keep praising."

Oh thank You, Lord, You are mighty to get the message through the mashed potatoes, the dogs barking, laughter, and stories—even the dishes and garbage.

Darkness has to flee in the light of His presence, for we are blessed because we know the joyful sound. Keep laughing—even if the jokes are on me!

We're filling up the soul's U-Haul!

22

The Gift

It was 1977. A blizzard swept through January like a roaring lion. Greensboro, North Carolina was encased in ice. Trees in the forest crashed into the woods with a sound like gunfire; branches laden with ice cracked in the wind. Harold piled logs on the porch, and we prayed for the power lines to hold fast.

Dr. Bruce pulled into the driveway in his Jeep. "Just stopped by for a cup of tea."

"Thank you, dear." Mama's beautiful smile shone through her pale face like golden sunshine.

A truck pulled up. "Brought you some good mountain air, Mama—makes breathing easier." The men rolled in the extra oxygen tanks in case the roads became impassable. "Thank you, dear."

A strong hand wiped a tear. "What a gal! What a gal!"

Harold kept the fireplace filled with blazing logs.

Grace, our faithful organizing sister, stayed on the telephone checking airlines or buses for the arrival of the other sisters— Joyce from Chicago, Jeanelle from Florida. They had been rerouted and met in an out-of-the-way airport where they ran into each other exclaiming, "How did you get here?"

"Grace called and said to come home. Mama is much weaker." Jeanelle, dressed in a Florida wardrobe, shivered in the cold.

In the early morning a cab from Raleigh pulled into our driveway. "Mama, the girls are here."

"Thank you, dear."

Doris put on the coffeepot.

The upstairs rooms looked like a dormitory with four sisters catching up on news.

I had the night watch. Harold kept the logs blazing.

The weary travelers, warm and fed, fell asleep. The wind howled while icy branches cracked in the night.

I dozed beside Mama's bed, with the sound of oxygen bubbling in the tank. Mama rested peacefully. Her children were home. She was safe.

I held the hand that had taken a scrub brush to do what she had to do. I stroked the hand that had rocked the babies, fed the hungry, kneaded the dough for the whole wheat bread. (The end slices were my favorite, and one day I sliced the ends of five loaves of bread—and ate them all dripping with butter.) While those hands stirred the oatmeal Mama told us we would not go hungry. We didn't!

"Oatmeal three times a day keeps the hunger away."

Now the hand tinged with blue would not hold her beloved Bible anymore. She had read it through three times during the past year, but we took turns to read where she had stopped. No one dared to miss the "begats" or the "judgments for disobedience"; we had to read every verse.

I had bathed her, rubbed her with lotion, cut her toenails; Joyce trimmed her fingernails and curled her hair. We wrapped a pink shawl around her shoulders. The pink satin slippers were under the bed.

Her feet wouldn't wear her pink slippers, but soon she'd wear golden slippers all over God's Heaven. Mama was going Home!

I heard Joyce in the kitchen, always the faithful one to serve. Grace now took her turn in the chair while I went to bed. We heard her singing, "He the pearly gates will open." I was too tired to realize the humor of Grace singing. She was the organist—not a soloist.

Throughout the day we took turns reading Scripture and singing the old hymns. The sisters took turns at the piano; songs of faith filled the house with the sound of joy. This was not the time to grieve. Tears would come later.

Around the bed we gathered, the five daughters, and we thanked our Mama for the blessing she had been to us. "I will meet you in the morning, just inside the eastern gate."

"Thank you, dear." (This time I think she meant Jesus.)

We did thank Him for the gift of His love for us all, the gift of salvation, the gift of faith, and the gift of love for each other.

The blizzard hemmed us in! The wind roared through the frozen trees. The logs blazed in the fireplace.

The power lines held. The coffeepot kept perking, and Joyce always managed to prepare tasty snacks, even when we said we weren't hungry. We ate!

Once again it was my turn to sleep. Suddenly it was 7 P.M. and I was wide awake. We gathered around our mother and sang, "I will meet you in the morning."

Ralph came in, leaned over, and kissed her cheek. "It's Ralph, Grandma."

"Praise the Lord."

Within a few minutes—7:30 P.M., January 14, 1977—Mama went Home peacefully, surrounded by her children—and the angels.

We stood and sang the doxology. God had given us a gift—the honor of ushering her into His presence.

Tears came later, for the memories that bless and burn and that "lonesome, missing you kind of feeling."

Now it was January 1997, 20 years later. I sat in my kitchen, bowed in grief over my sister Grace who was no longer able to care for herself in the retirement home in Greensboro, North Carolina, 200 miles away from Wilmington where Jeanelle and I lived. "God, please show me what to do. I want to do Your will."

Quietly, like a gentle breeze, the familiar words came through: "I will instruct you and teach you in the way you shall go; I will guide you with My eye."

"Thank You, Lord. Now what is the next step?"

"Bring her home to you."

I grabbed the phone. "Joyce, don't fly to Greensboro. Come here instead, and I'll make plans to bring her home to me."

"Oh, I was so troubled—couldn't sleep all night—and now I have peace. This is right."

I called the doctor, the retirement home, and Hospice, and within a short time plans were on the table. In the meantime Jeanelle was in a prayer group and sensed the same message: "Bring Grace home."

I called Jan. "Oh, Mother, this is God's gift to you all—a gift of love. You promised to love each other and care for each other—so this is a gift."

I called Ralph. "Mom, it is right, and we will all help."

Peace, peace, wonderful peace, coming down from the Father above.

Jeanelle was on the phone with Doris's children, Davidson and Doreen. They would bring Grace home—to me.

It was Sunday! We all came home from church and sat down to Sunday dinner. We prayed for the travelers from Greensboro, bringing Grace home to a safe place.

"They are here!"

All the family ran to the door, and I stood holding the door open while strong men held Grace. I shook with sobs—just for a moment. *This is my sister! My beautiful, New York Fifth-Avenue fashion dresser; the capable secretary to Dr. McQuilkin at Columbia Bible College; the traveler who lived in Switzerland working in the Billy Graham conference; the musician.*

"My sister!"

Ralph put his arms around me. "Wipe your tears, Mom. Don't let her see you cry. It is a gift."

Loving arms sat her in a chair, surrounded by family—sisters, nieces, and nephews—and friends. Like sunshine after rain, a gentle smile filled her pale face. "Thank you."

"I will instruct you and teach you in the way you shall go"—and I knew each step would be ordered of the Lord.

Our beloved friend, Dr. Luke Sampson, came over to see Grace. We gathered in the living room, and he heard us sing. Jeanelle sat at the piano, and Joyce sang. Then we said, "Grace, we need to sing our theme song for Dr. Luke—the one the sisters love to belt out in whatever key."

> Born again
> There's been a change in me
> Born again
> Just as Jesus said
> Born again
> All because of Calvary
> I'm glad, so glad
> That I've been born again.

I watched Grace softly sing the words in her low key. God had given us all a gift.

When Joyce came from Arkansas she brought the Gaither videos along. We put Grace in a big chair, wrapped in a soft blanket, and Joyce turned on the music.

The musicians sang about Heaven, and Grace listened. "We are all going Home, Grace, and someday we will all be together."

Her smile was her answer.

In a few days I had to pack my bags again. "I just can't leave!"

"We'll manage fine. Chris is coming, and Hospice will help us." (I was learning more about this wonderful organization, Hospice.)

With bags packed I headed into zero weather for Omaha, Nebraska. At the banquet I said, "God has His mysterious ways of giving us gifts of love. We don't understand that the contents of life's barrel—the events of life we don't plan—are gifts.

"It is a time to show others around us the peace in the storm, the joy in sorrow, the love for each other—for all in the family of God, the weak and the strong. Lena would say, 'Take them by the hand and take them home.'

"Not only are the tests a gift, for the 'trials of our faith are more precious than gold'; the gift to us is bigger than that. It is a time to give God a gift, our gift of faith.

"Trust and obey, for there is no other way."

23

The Letter

Dear Eric,

I read a copy of the letter you wrote about forgiveness and believe me, you have learned a valuable lesson. From my view from the top of years I have seen how an unforgiving spirit opens the door for bitterness and resentment that can lead to anger and hatred.

You were so on target when you said that creativity freezes in an attitude of unforgiveness. Forgiveness is an act of the will and not a feeling. God's Word says to forgive as He forgives us.

Forgiveness is very difficult when we think we have a "reason" to hate. But God doesn't give the option; He gives the command.

Remember the story about Joseph, when his brothers sold him to the Egyptians, then lied to the father? All those years the old father thought his son was dead. In the meantime, God was teaching Joseph some valuable lessons, and he learned to forgive before he became prime minister of Egypt.

Reconciliation came later—but I must also tell you that reconciliation doesn't always follow. We forgive according to God's principles, and sometimes the other party couldn't care less—or may even be dead—but before God we forgive in obedience to Him and we are set free.

I have met people all shriveled up in bitterness who can't forgive something that happened 40 or 50 years ago. Can you imagine a lifetime of bitterness, when that person could be set free to allow all the creative potential to be developed? Creativity can't flow from a shriveled, bitter spirit.

I realize that you could have been filled with anger over the unfairness of a situation, but you didn't allow it to master you. Remember, you can do all things through Christ who strengthens you—and you chose to forgive. Good for you!

Pride goes before a fall, but let me tell you that an unforgiving spirit opens the door to every evil thing. That is also true about an unthankful spirit.

Remember how the children of Israel didn't do anything that bad at first—just griped a lot? Look where it led them—away from the true and living God, and then there was a generation that didn't know the Lord.

Spurgeon, the great preacher, said that having an unthankful spirit is like walking on the edge of a cliff, where one can slide into an abyss of any sin. Just think, Eric! An unthankful spirit can do all that damage! Keep your heart thankful, and the battle is in the will to forgive. We choose to obey God's rules for living.

Remember this—that all the redemptive power of God the Father, Jesus the Son, and the Holy Spirit operates on the track of obedience. God won't jump the track for anyone.

It is so simple—trust God and obey. Your great-grandmother would say, "Oh ja, it is so simple—just not so easy." It is hard to obey, but Eric, remember it is harder to disobey.

I'm so proud of you and God will bless you for your thankful and forgiving spirit. I'll be watching for all the God-given potential in you to "bust out all over"!

Love, Grammy

P.S. Enclosed find $20 to take Clover out and do something special. Give her my love.

24

The Engagement

"Grammy, did you get Eric's phone call?"

"Not yet, but he said he had something to tell me and would call."

"It's a surprise! He's asked Clover to marry him and he gave her a ring."

"So much for surprises when you are around, Katie. Believe me—no secrets in this family."

"Well, Grammy, just act surprised!"

I did! A phone call came later from Eric.

"I have news for you! I asked Clover to marry me and I gave her a ring."

I did my part—I acted surprised!

"I took Clover up on our favorite mountain trail and got down on my knees and asked her to marry me. I did everything right, Grammy. I asked her parents, also talked to my parents, and I talked to you some time ago."

"Well, what did she say?"

"Here—I'll let Clover tell you."

"I cried and cried and said, 'Yes, yes, yes!'"

"Good for you, Clover, and welcome into the family. We all love you, and I am proud of you and Eric. Just think—you've been together through four years of college, and you made good choices. You chose to love God and serve Him. You chose to accept Jesus Christ as your Savior and also to allow Him to be the Lord of your lives. You also chose to honor marriage as sacred before God, and you have chosen to honor your parents by listening to their wisdom. You also will find out that good choices build strong character and God will never fail you.

"Trust me. I've lived a long time, and it is true God is faithful and will guide you step by step. God bless you both!"

Eric came back on the phone. "What do you think about that, Grammy?"

"I think it is wonderful, Eric! Let me know when you set the date, and I will be sure to be there! Don't forget what I told you, Eric! Cherish Clover! She will respect you! That makes a good marriage.

"Remember all the letters I have written to you? Well, review them! Ha!

"Read Proverbs for everyday living; read Psalms to see what a big God we have. Read the Bible together. Pray together—*just do it!*

"Another thing, Eric. Don't make a decision without talking it over with Clover. Always listen to her and don't make a decision until you agree. Even if she is wrong, just pray for God to show her or you His plan. *Always* be agreed!

"Remember you are the head of the home, but Clover is your partner. Never allow anything to come between you. Settle any disagreement before night comes. Don't ever sleep on anger, but talk it out and let the love you have for each other rule in your hearts.

"Don't forget to have fun—and keep a sense of humor. You'll make it! You're getting a good start! God will complete what He started in you.

"Don't worry! I'll write it all down again. After all, your Papa and I lived together for 53 years, and we did learn a few good lessons to pass on to you 'youngsters.' Since you are such smart grandchildren I'm sure you'll listen.

"Anyhow, I love you and am proud of you both. Give Clover a big hug from me—that shouldn't be too difficult.

"I'll talk to you again. So long for now." I hung up the phone. It was quiet in the house.

I picked up the picture of Clover and Eric and prayed for God's blessing on these two special children.

Clover grew up in a pastor's home where she learned the basic principles of Christian life from her father, Jerry Musick, a Baptist minister. Debbie, her mother, is a lovely, gracious hostess who made us welcome as their guests. Tal, the younger brother, made Eric his hero, and they had long talks together.

Jerry's Bible teaching gave Clover and Eric godly principles, and there was great respect for Clover's minister father. "Eric is teachable," Jerry confided in me, "and I know he will grow spiritually. We've had some good conversations on Sunday afternoons."

I looked at the picture again. Clover, in a black sleeveless evening gown with her beautiful auburn curly hair framing her face, stood almost six feet tall beside Eric, six feet, six inches. What a striking couple!

Now plans were underway for a summer wedding, and Chris and I had to work on a wedding guest list. The rest of my sermons would have to wait—and I had a few on the backroads of my mind.

Tomorrow I'll get a frame for that picture.

25

Keep the Song

Sometimes I'm afraid! I know the Bible says, "Fear not," but I forget at times. For me, this is a "going Home time," just a few more miles of rocky roads, detours, and winding trails that seem to lead to nowhere. The tears come, but not the agonized weeping from my younger days.

I remember one time when I thought my heart would break, and I wept so hard I fell down in a gravel trail on a country road. I lay there, sobbing big, gulping sobs. Suddenly I stood up and said, "I'll never cry like that again. I just wept for anything or everything that should come to pass.

"Okay, Lord—that's it! I cried enough, so I'm telling You that the next time I face a crisis I will cry to You, but I won't choke on those sobs anymore. I'm going to sing more and cry less.

"Besides, it didn't change a thing. However, I feel better to let it all out.

"Lord, I'm glad You were the only one watching—and You won't tell."

There have been many times since that day when I have shed tears, weeping—but not that choking, sobbing kind that drains the life out and leaves a shaking body feeling hopeless and out of control. Now I cry to the Lord. He hears me! He really does!

Now when I am afraid I tell Him. "Oh Lord, I'm really afraid, but You said that the time I'm afraid I should trust You. Okay, Lord, I'm trusting You, that out of the darkness and confusion You will be there and that Your Word is a lamp and light."

He was there! He also said that I would learn a new song. Oh, I know Lena and I made up songs in the college infirmary, and we would sing to Lena's beat—songs of faith and victory.

Not all songs are in the major key; some are songs we learn in the night, haunting songs in a minor key. A new song is a song we learn in each time of testing, because it's not "one song fits all" but a new song each time.

In the night of sorrow there would come a soft lullaby of comfort like "peace, peace, wonderful peace." I know He was there. In a time of crisis sometimes there would come a rousing marching song: "Go out there! Possess the land!" In times of confusion and in that "all alone, lonesome feeling" would come a love song—a love song from Heaven: a "God so loved He gave" kind of song.

There would be times of anger (righteous indignation sounds better!) when I railed at the injustice abounding in our culture. There would come a song of "Standing on the Promises," like when the howling winds assail, God will prevail: "You, Margaret, just keep standing on the promises of God."

We don't need explanations! We need to stand on the promises. A new song! Every situation is different, but God gives a song, in the night season and all the day long.

I remember when I was visiting with Ruth Nelson in Gig Harbor at the Cottesmore Nursing Home. Inez Glass, the owner, was showing us the new Alzheimer's unit. Two women came toward us arm in arm, each holding a teddy bear in her other arm. They giggled like schoolgirls.

Ruth lifted up her accordion and started to play, "You Are My Sunshine." Our two "teddy bear" friends danced in glee and the quiet place came alive with music. Suddenly the heads that had been drooping lifted and feet started to keep a beat.

I read a story of how a loving daughter spent hours with her mother, an Alzheimer's patient, singing old familiar love songs. The world around the mother had slipped away. The song remained.

When I called a loved one who lived in a world of confused thoughts I'd say, "Let's sing!"

"Oh yes, let's sing!"

Our favorite was, "Surely goodness and mercy shall follow me all the days of my life." Then I would hear her harmonize in perfect key:

And I shall dwell
In the house of the Lord forever
And I shall feast at the
Table spread for me.

"Oh, isn't it wonderful, that someday we will be Home—all together?"

"Oh yes! Let's sing!" That was a new song in the night.

I read an incredible story that someone sent to me. I have no idea where my unknown friend found it.

It was Christmas Eve, 1875. Ira D. Sankey was traveling by steamboat up the Delaware River. It was a calm, starlit evening, and there were many passengers gathered on deck. Mr. Sankey was asked to sing. He stood, leaning against one of the great funnels of the boat, and his eyes were raised to the starry heavens in quiet prayer. It was his intention to sing a Christmas song, but he was driven almost against his will to sing "Saviour, Like a Shepherd Lead Us."

There was deep stillness. Words and melody, welling forth from the singer's soul, floated out over the deck and the quiet river. Every heart was touched.

After the song ended, a man with a rough, weather-beaten face came up to Mr. Sankey and said, "Did you ever serve in the Union army?"

"Yes," answered Mr. Sankey, "beginning in the spring of 1860."

"Can you remember if you were doing picket duty on a bright, moonlit night in 1862?"

"Yes," answered Mr. Sankey, very much surprised.

"So did I," said the stranger, "but I was serving in the Confederate army. When I saw you standing at your post I said to myself, 'That fellow will never get away from here alive.' I raised my musket and took aim. I was standing in the shadow, completely concealed, while the full light of the moon was falling upon you. At that instant, just as a moment ago, you raised your eyes to Heaven and began to sing. Music, especially song, has always had a wonderful power over me, and I took my finger off the trigger.

"'Let him sing his song to the end,' I said to myself. 'I can shoot him afterwards. He's my victim in any event, and my bullet cannot miss him.' But the song you sang then was the song you sang just now. I heard the words perfectly: 'We are Thine, do Thou befriend us, be the Guardian of our way.'

"When you had finished your song it was impossible for me to take aim at you again. I thought, 'The Lord, who is able to save that man from certain death, must surely be great and mighty,' and my arm, of its own accord, dropped limp at my side.

"Since that time I have wandered about, far and wide, but when I just now saw you standing there praying as on that other occasion, I recognized you. Then my heart was wounded by your song. Now I ask that you help me find a cure for my sick soul."

Deeply moved, Mr. Sankey threw his arms about the man who in the days of the war had been his enemy. And that night the stranger found the Good Shepherd as his Saviour.

Blessed is the people that know the joyful sound: they shall walk, O Lord, in the light of thy countenance" (Psalm 89:15).

Sing!

26

The Tea Cup

With the mail came a package from Gracie, the daughter of my long-ago friend who went Home. When I opened the carefully wrapped gift I saw a beautiful blue tea cup and saucer.

The note read:

I know that you and Mom were good friends for many years, and I have pictures of you both. Enclosed is a cup and saucer and a small crystal plate for cookies. Remember Mom—especially when you read *First We Have Coffee*.

A tug came on the heart and quiet tears fell. Almost 60 years of friendship came tumbling into that blue cup—memories of nursing days, weddings, and births. Gladys Thompson Ellefsen went Home, but she left her poetry and music in the lives of her children, who continue to teach the biblical lessons to their children. If tea cups could talk, what stories would pour out!

I looked at the shelf that held the tiny demitasse cups and saucers that Harold brought as a "special surprise." (I must remember to give them to the grandchildren.)

Somehow the memory of "us sisters" drinking coffee or tea came in to fill every cup on the shelf. Jeanelle liked to serve a different delicate china cup to each one of us. Doris kept the coffeepot on and sturdy mugs held more than a tea cup. We'd carry our mugs out on the patio and watch the sun set over the Blue Ridge mountains of North Carolina.

Joyce treasured the blue Danish cups from Grandma Jensen, but when she served pancakes on Saturday morning to her Sunday school class, the mugs stood in a row.

Out of those tea cups come the memories of songs. Sometimes tears fill the cup, but always the triumphant sound of joy would come through the valley of life's valuable lessons.

We were all there when we served Mama her last cup of tea in a china cup, then watched her bow her head in thanks. "Thanks" was her life—even over the cup of tea. "Love each other and take care of each other," were her words before she went Home.

Strange how a tea cup could stir up memories. On my kitchen shelf is an old melmac cup from Mama's "everyday" set. She thought it was beautiful, and now I use it as a measuring cup.

Out of the tea cups come the memories of triumph and failure, joys and sorrows; but when we come together—*we sing*!

One morning as we sat around the table with our mugs of coffee, my grandson was getting ready to head for the beach. I kept waiting for him to leave so we could get on with our stories, but he called me aside. Wistfully he asked, "Could I join you and hear your stories? You have so much fun." He took a mug and joined the great aunts and Grandma.

We often wonder if we are teaching the children well and whether our words of wisdom will be remembered. It took me some time to learn that we were teaching the younger generation how to enjoy each other.

When we brought our frail sister Grace to Wilmington to get ready to go Home, she was surrounded by her sisters. She looked up at Joyce and asked, "Will you be here when the time comes?"

"We will all be here!"

When Shawn said, "I want to take care of my sisters and brother like that," I knew life's valuable lessons were coming through with the clarity of a "visual aid lesson."

Grace was peaceful, surrounded by loving care. Doctor and staff said, "We have never seen such love." Mama must be watching from her view from the top.

A tug on my heart reminds me that one cup will be missing. But the love and memories will sustain us, no matter how many tea cups are missing. We will all be together someday—Home!

Last night, after a delightful evening dining with new friends Jim, Jodi, and Henry at the Oceanic overlooking the ocean, I was given a gift—a book titled *Sisters*. This morning I held the book in my hand and couldn't put it down.

The essays are written by Carol Saline, and the magnificent photography is by Sharon J. Wahlmuth. Turning the pages I see the very young sisters, then the teens, beautiful young women. But what caught my attention was the picture of the invalid sister in a chair, with a colorful

Afghan around her. Beside her sat the 86-year-old sister, bent with weariness but sustained by love.

The black faces reflected pain, sorrow, and the storms of life, but through the storm came peace. "The good Lord takes care of me, and I take care of my sister."

There was a time when we were all eating in a restaurant and someone approached us as we were laughing and telling stories. "Are you sisters or are you friends? I just lost my sister and there is no one to share the memories." A tea cup was missing.

Jeanelle answered, "We were born sisters, but we chose each other for friends." Somehow we stay forever children when retelling the stories of childhood.

Oh Father, let us show your strength and power to the next generation.

At one of the women's retreats a woman came to me to tell her story. "I have mix-and-match dishes with chipped places. When I read your book *First We Have Coffee* and saw the picture of tea cups, I longed for a pretty tea cup, but finances were on zero.

"One day I received a gift—a beautiful tea cup and saucer. I hid it in my dresser, in a safe place.

"When the strain of frugal living scratches on the soul, I go to the dresser and reach for my tea cup. Quietly I sit alone and sip my coffee from a beautiful cup and thank God for the small pleasures that soothe the soul."

> P.S. Thank you for the gift of a tea cup filled with memories of a long-ago friend.
>
> Thank you for the book that makes me relive the years of living that only sisters share.

27

The Last Brick

The majestic strains of the processional filled the magnificent Gordon College Chapel. Men and women who had driven the stakes of their faith into the fabric of this New England community moved steadily to the marching beat. Dr. Judson Carlberg, the president and my son-in-love, marched with me at the end of the line.

When we stood to sing "Great Is Thy Faithfulness" I caught Chad's eye, seated beside Jan, his mother. In front of me sat the graduating class, some 15 of whom from the Frisbee team had slept in my garage or office. Today they looked older and wiser.

Then it was my turn! What does an 80-year-old grandmother tell graduates who are crammed full of knowledge and technology for a new century?

If I could have gathered them as a mother hen protecting her chicks, I would have done it. I wanted to shield them from a world hostile to their faith.

They weren't here in this beautiful setting to be shielded but to be fortified with armor to go out and stand against the foe; but more than that, to stand *for the truth*.

I recalled how I had been awakened in the darkness of an early dawn in the forest of Northern California—and now I was standing before this audience with the message that came to me in that early morning. I told them the story of "The Last Brick."

This story says that off the rocky coast of England was a dangerous shoal called "Dead Man's Cove," where cliffs rose majestically out of the sea. Treacherous currents swept boats that came too close, to dash them against the rocks.

One day a fishing boat did just that—came too close and was dashed against the rocks. Since the fisherman was an excellent swimmer, he knew he could make it to the cliff, where there was a ledge of safety. With great effort he made it to the cliff, only to find that the tide and time had washed the cliff smooth like slippery glass. *There was nothing to hold onto!* The fisherman was lost.

A young minister heard the story and drove iron stanchions into the cliff, with a rope attached to the ledge of safety. From then on, no one would be lost for lack of a stronghold.

I told the students, "When I heard the story I wondered how many have lost their way in the treacherous currents of the slippery cliff called life. When I watch young people sliding into an abyss of despair, huddled together with no stanchions to hold to—and no rope—I wonder if they will be dashed against the rocks.

"A young man told me, 'We have been put out to pasture with no fences. I'm sure we would jump the fences, but we would know there was a fence to come back to.'

"I pondered what the iron stanchions to hold onto would be, while preparing to enter into the new century. What are the ABC's of life?

"A: The 'at-one-ment,' where God and man meet at the cross, the pivot upon which time and eternity turns. The death, burial, and resurrection of Jesus gave us a Savior. Without the resurrection we would honor a prophet or a teacher—but not a Redeemer.

"If our vessel is broken from our moorings in Christ Jesus, the Son of God, the Deity, we will be dashed against the rocks and carried out to a sea of deadly error. We can do without theories, but we can't do without the Christ of the cross—and the resurrection! Jesus said, 'I am the way, the truth, and the life; no man comes to the Father but by me.'

"B: The battle to believe! The trial of our faith is more precious than gold. Worldly ease snaps the sinews of sacred courage. The battle to believe is fought in the arena of the will. When the heart is fixed, the feet will be established.

"The Holy Spirit is God's processing power who enables us to live out the life of Christ in the marketplace. We are all in full-time Christian service.

"Through living out our Christian faith we can greatly draw others from the unholy arena of hostility to faith into the holy presence of God.

"C: Choices—we rivet our chains by our choices. The choice is obedience to God's standards—not to change the godly principles to fit the world's standards, but to change the standards to fit God's laws into our culture.

"Methods may change, but godly principles remain like the Alps, not affected by the wind. So the cross stands towering o'er the wrecks of time.

"You graduates of Gordon College are not left to be dashed against the rocks; you have a current to plug into, iron stanchions to hold, and fences to return to.

"Godly men and women have been laying the iron stakes of their faith into this community. A. J. Gordon, the founder, was a man with the forward look and the upward look—no turning back. The battle is in the will. You must choose: 'I have decided to follow Jesus.'

"C. S. Lewis says that 'history will reveal that the Christians who did the most for the present world were those who thought most about the next.' We must not forget that this is 'on-the-job training' for when we rule and reign with Him.

"Across the Market Place in Savannah, Georgia, stands a church built by former slaves. After long hours of toil, they built bonfires for light to work at night, and the women carried bricks in their aprons. Not much has been recorded, but one statement stands out. The man who laid the first brick also laid the last brick—four years later.

> Lord, haste the day
> When the faith shall be sight,
> The clouds be rolled back as a scroll.
> The trump shall resound
> And the Lord shall descend. . . .

"What will He say? 'Even so, it is well with Gordon College!'

"A. J. Gordon laid the first brick, but Gordon students going out into the marketplace will lay the last brick!

"Finish well!"

28

The Language of Love

When Eric was about five years old he drew a picture of me walking on a rope that ended someplace in the sky. Shawn, much wiser and older, dared to ask, "What in the world is that?"

"That is Grammy going to Heaven."

"That is stupid! I don't want Grammy going anyplace."

"Oh, I know—she's not going yet. I just want her to know that I know where she is going."

I kept that picture on a cup, right on my kitchen windowsill.

On my 80th birthday I was given the book by Joni Eareckson Tada, *Heaven*. Now that tells me something! It's a beautiful book, by the way, and it is nice to know something about your next home.

The language of love comes in many forms. Looking back over the years I see things from a different viewpoint and remember the language of love that didn't come with words.

On Saturday night my father polished the shoes for Sunday morning. Six pair stood in a row, ready for the trek to Sunday school.

Now I view them not just as polished shoes heading off to Sunday school, but also as the shoes that sent us on our walk of faith.

In between harshness and discipline came the language of love that sometimes gets lost in a hurried world. The memory of my father shaking the stove at 5:30 A.M. and singing "Standing on the Promises," giving me that extra half hour to crawl under the quilt, is still vivid.

"Get up, Margaret!" may have sounded harsh, but the warm kitchen was a language without words. Six slices of oven toast and mugs of hot cocoa were on a plate.

I said, "Thank you" and bundled up for my long walk to Carl Schurz High School. Now I wish I had said more to let him know I understood love without words.

When I tell Katie these stories I try to remind her to be thankful for the small deeds. "In looking back, Katie, it is not the big crises of life that topple us as trees of righteousness, but the everyday irritations that hack away at the soul."

One day when I was troubled about what motivated someone to do a certain act, Jan quietly said, "Don't trouble yourself with other people's motives—only deal with the actual need! Only God knows the motives of the heart."

One Sunday at the dining room table I told a Valentine story. When I was about seven years old my mother bought me a large pink heart for Valentine's Day.

I was thrilled! A store-bought Valentine! No one ever had a store-bought valentine! Through the years I treasured that Valentine and kept it in a safe place. Before

Mama died, I mentioned how I treasured the big pink heart, and she told me a story.

"Ja, ja," she said softly, "I remember how Mrs. Magnusen loved you and always wanted you to spend the night with her two daughters. You were so excited to go there because there were beautiful dolls to play with, and she also had fancy food that we couldn't afford."

Mama continued her story quietly. "I thought I was losing you and you loved Mrs. Magnusun more than me, so I had to do something to show you how much I loved you."

"Oh, Mama, how could you think that?"

"Ja, I know. I just thought of all the lovely things they gave you, and all I could do was to make everything from something old. So this one time I would buy a store-bought Valentine. I saved the pennies and finally had enough to buy a heart Valentine."

"Oh, Mama, how I treasured that pink heart all the years. But Mother dear, you were always the most beautiful, wonderful mother in all the world to me."

"Ja, I guess it was foolish to think that things could make a difference."

When I finished the story everyone was quiet around the table. "Don't forget to be thankful for the love that comes to us in a language without words. Sometimes I think when I get to Heaven I'll want to hug my father and thank him for the polished shoes, the warm kitchen, and the oven toast—and I'll even remember to thank my Mama for the pink heart Valentine."

The days passed quickly until we gathered again around the table. Chad gave me a valentine. "Grammy, I went all over town to find a big pink heart; couldn't find it, so this red one will have to do."

Katie wrote a note: "You don't have to buy a pink Valentine for me. I'll always know how much you love me."

One day I stood before another graduating class, at Endicott College, and concluded with this story:

A graduating student had looked at cars with his father and had picked a color and design. With great expectations the student was honored at a graduation party.

His father presented him with a gift—a Bible. "In here are the treasures of life." The son threw the Bible down and ran away from home in anger.

Years later he returned at his father's death and found the Bible in the father's possessions. He opened the Bible, and there was the check for the new car.

I looked out at the sea of faces before me. "In this Book you will find God's language of love. Don't miss it!"

29

Grace

Across the hills and valley the snow fell while the wind whipped the canopy over the open grave. Down the road Mama's yellow house stood guard. On the hill the colonial home of the Hammers looked across the road to the family cemetery where Papa, Mama, Gordon, and Gordon's wife Alice were buried. From the lovely home on Eagle Ridge had come the sound of music through the years. It was a place of refuge from life's storms and joyous celebrations when the children, Doreen, Donald, Davidson, Duane, and their families gathered.

Doris and I often walked the country roads and shared our dreams of a safe place for our children to gather. Today we gathered to honor the memory of Grace, the second sister to go Home. Bernice, only two years old, died from diphtheria when Grace was born. I had stood by the window and said, "God made an exchange. He took Bernice but gave us Grace."

A church bus from Greensboro came around the bend, and strong hands helped the Sunday school teacher and friends to be seated with the family under the canopy.

Peter Stam's clear voice sounded out against the wind: "The Lord is my shepherd . . . and I shall dwell in the house of the Lord forever."

The graves were silent, but I knew there was rejoicing in Heaven. Earth's journey was finished.

Reverend Jon Estes, the beloved pastor of Rocky Knoll Baptist Church, where Grace was a member, spoke of the blessing that she had been to their church. "Her faithful witness, encouragement, and beautiful smile will always be with us."

The faithful Sunday school class had been her "sisters" when we were separated by miles. There were no words to express our deepest thanks to these precious people who had been her family during the years in Greensboro.

"I can't believe that you dear ones came in this stormy weather!"

"We loved her!"

We told them how we brought Grace to my home in Wilmington from Greensboro—200 miles away—and how happy she was to be in a safe place, with her sisters around her.

"Everyone loved her at Village Green Retirement Home, where she played the piano for vespers, worked in the gift shop, and in her quiet, gentle way tended to the needs of other residents."

Someone else added, "*Everyone* thought she was Grace's 'best friend.'" Pastor Estes, a faithful pastor and friend, added that he always came away encouraged by Grace.

We continued our story so her friends would know about her last days. "We took care of her at home, and she listened to Gaither videos. We sang and played the piano and kept her comfortable. She had no pain!

"When a newly furnished nursing home was ready, Grace was one of the first patients, and needless to say, she was loved by the staff and Hospice.

"A dear friend and beloved physician, Dr. Luke Sampson, cared for Grace; he also joined with us in song and prayer. Joyce stayed with her most of the day, but Jeanelle and I came and we all prayed together.

"On February 7, 1997, I felt an urgency to see Grace, so I dressed early, and Joyce and I drank our coffee. Dr. Luke called to let us know there had been a change. Then we called Jeanelle and Peter.

"Our friends nodded and listened as Joyce told how Grace had asked her, 'Will you be there when the time comes?'

" 'We will all be here!'

"We were there!

"Joyce whispered in her ear, 'Remember when I longed for a Shirley Temple doll? When Christmas came, there was my doll. I combed her hair. Thank you, Grace.'

"I reminded her how she finished a sewing project for me after I messed it up. 'Thank you, Grace.'

"By that time she didn't respond, but tears slipped down her cheeks. She knew we were there."

The friends on that church bus listened, and we promised to come and tell the Sunday school class how Grace went Home.

"We sang the old hymns of faith, and the staff watched and joined their tears with ours—Lori, Roxanna, and others. Dr. Luke Sampson slipped in, then Ralph came, and while Peter Stam was quoting the 23rd Psalm, Horace and Tennie Hilton joined us.

"We watched Grace go Home while singing 'He the Pearly Gates Will Open.'

"We kept our promise! We were there!"

We watched the church bus leave, with the falling snow covering the graves. It was a time when the family shared their personal memories over Doreen's pound cake and hot coffee.

Then it was time for us to leave Stoneville, North Carolina, and head back to Wilmington. Cards and letters keep coming, reminding us about a life well spent—a faithful servant.

Someone from Columbia Bible College days, when Grace was Dr. McQuilkin's right-arm secretary and assistant, told how Dr. McQuilkin would walk briskly to an engagement, Grace with pen and notebook keeping step.

Somehow I just imagined Dr. McQuilkin at the Pearly Gates: "Well, well, Grace. Welcome Home, faithful servant." (She is probably stepping right along, taking notes.)

What a reunion with loved ones! Now Grace and Bernice are together. The cross took away the sting of death—they are alive forever more!

When Grace lived in Switzerland, while with the Billy Graham mission conference, she spoke of the beauty of the mountains and valleys. We heard from others about her organizational skills. How she loved music—the organ and the piano!

From her view from the top she knows the reality of her life's verse—not only for her, but for us who are still climbing the road to Home. "And God is able to make all grace abound toward you; that ye, always having all sufficiency in all things, may abound to every good work" (2 Corinthians 9:8).

P.S. Joyce prayed with two of the staff members of the nursing home and they, too, came to receive God's grace—the gift of salvation through Jesus Christ.

30

The Day the Steeple Fell

I clipped the headlines from the Wilmington *Star-News* and read that the 197-foot steeple of the First Baptist Church lay in a pile of red brick and copper. During the night of Hurricane Fran, 1996, a thunderous crash was heard and the steeple that had withstood previous storms for 130 years now crashed to the ground. The "Beacon of Faith! Monument to Tenacity" made the headlines.

The pastor spoke of how each generation stands on the shoulders of generations before them, and that history and heritage would be honored again. If I know anything about this community, the steeple will rise again.

Down the corridors of my imagination I wondered for a moment what the steeple, a beacon of faith, could see from the view from the top.

For 130 years this steeple had viewed wars and depressions, cultural upheavals, hurricanes, and storms; not just storms that brought havoc to the structure of brick and wood but those that brought havoc to the structure of families.

It is not the steeple that makes the difference in our culture, but it is a symbol of the faith of a people who make the difference.

The hurricane has taken its toll in destruction, but what about other storms that have taken their toll in the devastating winds lashed against the faith of our fathers—the faith symbolized by that steeple?

Crosses are taken down, nativity scenes removed from the Christmas season, Bible and prayer removed from our culture, as are the Ten Commandments, the foundation of law and social order.

What could go wrong in one generation? In my day students stood before a principal for throwing spitballs; today students stand before a judge for murder and rape.

I read someplace that man can tear down the church steeples but cannot tear the stars out of place. God still has His picture-book for us to view.

During my lifetime of depressions, wars, death, loss, broken dreams, God's people still stood on the promises of God. The mobs of the world still cry, "Crucify Him," but with other people of faith I cling to the old rugged cross, so despised by the world, and in that cross I glory, towering o'er the wrecks of time.

The Alps are not disturbed by the winds; even so the cross is not changed by the changing winds of a changing culture.

Malcolm Muggeridge said, "If the world were encased in concrete, there would be a crack; from that crack, the voice of the people of God." Our culture has been encased in concrete of disobedience to God's laws, and we reap the whirlwind. The power of the tyranny of hate built the Berlin Wall; the power of the prayer of God's people came through the cracks. The wall came down!

Seventy years of Marxism brought the downfall of a people who had been betrayed by the false gods of the tyranny of hate. From Christian schools and churches, 70 years of obedience to God's laws have sent leaders in every walk of life around the world—not to tear down, but to build churches, schools, hospitals. Not only have they built institutions, but they have also encouraged individuals to walk in God's ways, and built the family structure and great institutions of faith.

What made the difference in 70 years? One nation put faith in godless Marxism and burned the Book. Our nation sent people of faith in the Book to bring light into dark places, hope into despair. Christianity is not just a new way to live, but a new life to begin to live.

From the steeple, held high for 130 years, the view from the top could see the faith of our fathers and mothers living still, in spite of dungeon, fire, or sword.

I know this town will rally to build the steeple, a land-mark of faith. What will the new steeple see?

Robert Bork says, "It is significant that religion was seen as secure and central to American life in the nine-teenth century, but has appeared increasingly problematic and peripheral in the twentieth." Will the new steeple see the faith of our fathers and mothers return to recognize that the principles of Christianity and Judaism provide the major premise of moral reasoning by revelations and by the stories of the Bible?

We read in the Old Testament that there was a generation that did not know the Lord. Why? The children of Israel were encouraged to tell the stories to their children. They failed!

Joshua instructed the priests to take a stone from the River Jordan according to the tribes; that would be a sign when their children asked, "What are those stones?" Then they would tell how God parted the waters, and Joshua and the children of Israel walked over safely. This would be a memorial to the faithfulness of God.

God has recorded the stories in His Book, the Bible. From my view from the top I have tried to recall the stories of faith to leave for my grandchildren; not for them alone, but for the generations to come. Someday I will be Home!

The new steeple will rise into the next century, and what we see now can only change if we continue to tell the story of Jesus and His love.

In a paper I picked up from Gordon College, President Carlberg writes: "The problem is that important segments of Western culture have lost faith in what used to be a given in our civilization—that at the heart of human experience there is such a thing as truth."

We must pass on to the next generation that Jesus Christ is the Truth, the Life, the Way. The Truth is a person and personal—His life, death, and resurrection!

If the new steeple could look down on a nation that called out to God for forgiveness, then we could see the faith of our fathers and mothers moving into the next century.

While I was writing the final pages of this book I received a call from Jim Warren of *Prime Time America*, a talk show: "6 P.M.—we are on the air with your book, *A Nail in a Sure Place.*" When I reached for my book on the shelf I read again the introduction. "Men return again and again to the few who have mastered the spiritual secret, whose life has been hid with Christ, in God. These are of the old time religion, hung on the nails of the cross" (Robert Murry McCheyne, regarding Oswald Chambers). As I travel across the country I draw strength from the faithful people of God who "hang in there," nails fastened by God.

We must still go forth to be the music in a discordant world, the river in a dry place, the love in a world of hate and fear.

Before we go into a new century where the winds blow against our faith, we must kneel once more at Calvary. Behind our obedience to God is the reality of the cross— the cross beam of our faith.

"Then sings my soul, my Savior God, to Thee; how great Thou art."

P.S. I turned to my Bible, stained with tears and full of markings. I read again Psalm 71:18: "Now also when I am old and greyheaded, O God, forsake me not; until I have shewed thy strength unto this generation, and thy power to every one that is to come."

Other Books by
Margaret Jensen

All God's Children Got Robes

Filled with poignant and often humorous stories, Jensen relates her personal experience with cancer to powerfully illustrate God's faithfulness and provision. With her special gift of sharing and warm sense of humor, *All God's Children Got Robes* will encourage you in your faith.

First We Have Coffee

Margaret's warm stories of life as the daughter of a Scandinavian pastor in the Canadian north will touch your heart with timeless lessons of unwavering faith and family love. Margaret's mother is an indomitable character whose stern Norwegian discipline is matched only by her laughter and singing. The down-to-earth wisdom she passes on to both young and old over steaming cups of coffee will bring encouragement and hope to anyone who has gone through difficult times.

Lena

Margaret shares how she found a deeper relationship with God than she could have imagined through the exuberant, unshakable faith of a woman named Lena. Lena's strong, simple faith—her stories, songs, and laughter—will capture your heart and help you praise God until the joy comes.

A Nail in a Sure Place

Drawing on vibrant, real-life experiences, Margaret paints a colorful picture of God's sovereignty and provision. *A Nail in a Sure Place* will refresh your spirit and help you realize the power of God's love and faithfulness. These lively stories are perfect for encouraging your friends and for sharing the security and hope found in Jesus.